ADDICTIONS
COUNSELING

ADDICTIONS COUNSELING

A Practical Guide to Counseling People with Chemical and Other Addictions

Dianne Doyle Pita

Foreword by William Van Ornum

Crossroad | *New York*

1994

The Crossroad Publishing Company
370 Lexington Avenue, New York, NY 10017

Copyright © 1992 by Dianne Doyle Pita
Foreword Copyright © 1992 by William Van Ornum

Printed in the United States of America

Library of Congress Cataloging-in-Publication Data

Pita, Dianne Doyle.
Addictions counseling : a practical guide to counseling people
with chemical and other addictions / Dianne Doyle Pita ; foreword
by William Van Ornum.
p. cm.
Includes bibliographical references.
ISBN 0-8264-0543-6 (cloth); 0-8245-1386-X (pbk.)
1. Substance abuse—Patients—Counseling of. I. Title.
II. Series.
[DNLM: 1. Counseling—methods. 2. Substance Dependence-
-prevention & control. WM 270 P681a]
RC564.P58 1992
616.86′061—dc20
DNLM/DLC
for Library of Congress 91-20627
CIP

Contents

Acknowledgments

I wish to thank my family for their love and support: George, Ben, and Matthew; my friend and mentor, Carol Guild, for her wisdom and humor; Dr. John J. Shea for his broader perspective; my colleagues for sharing their expertise; and, especially, the clients and students whose courage and enthusiasm keep me striving to find a better way.

Finally, I want to thank Michael Leach and The Crossroad Publishing Company for recognizing the need to educate professional helpers on the process of recovery from addiction.

Foreword

Addictions Counseling brings a wealth of information to counselors. Even experienced professional therapists will learn a great deal from this book. Many of them have not had advanced training in working with chemical dependency and this book provides the knowledge needed to help persons who abuse various substances ranging from alcohol to cocaine to prescription drugs to other forms of chemical abuse. Dianne Doyle Pita recognizes the similarity in all forms of chemical dependency yet acknowledges issues that may arise with certain groups, such as physicians or nurses who abuse prescription drugs and may have ready access to these at their place of employment.

Empathy, a vital ingredient to all counseling, is needed when dealing with people who abuse substances, but also important is a knowledge of various states of addictions so that the counselor can make effective confrontations. While warmth and concern and sensitivity are needed, Dr. Pita stresses that "a major difference in treating addictions is the necessary condition of an active, direct, didactic approach with a clear plan of action. This approach is necessary in the early stages of counseling: assessing the problem, helping the client see that the chemical is the problem and helping him stop using the substance." The author provides a definition of substance abuse and describes general characteristics of the different stages of addiction, information that is useful to all helpers.

There is a saying in the counseling field that people "only reach out for help when they are ready." When working with substance abuse, many ask about the role of "coercion." Dr. Pita emphasizes that "practically all addicted individuals enter treat-

9

ment because they have been pushed by others to do so," and her ideas regarding interventions will assist families, employers, and counselors.

Many readers will have in their mind the question, "Is Alcoholics Anonymous by itself what is needed to treat substance abuse?" The author provides a detailed analysis of types of therapy, such as cognitive therapy or psychodynamic therapy, and discusses what these can add to the standard regimen of A.A. meetings. She recognizes that many individuals in treatment will be working with a team of persons (physician, counselor, psychologist, family therapist, etc.) and that they may try to "split" and antagonize the individuals against each other. Ways to prevent this are discussed. On the complementary role of A.A. and psychotherapy, she writes: "I remind my clients that even Bill W. (a founder of A.A.) was in psychotherapy."

An excellent section of the book pertains to ethics. It is important for helpers to keep clear the boundaries between themselves and their clients. Many in the helping fields are "co-dependent" personalities and this book discusses ways to combat the negative effects that a co-dependent orientation may have on the clients one serves.

Recently a split has occurred between many who work within the A.A. model and proponents of a cognitive therapy approach to addictions, and with hopes of helping the greatest number of individuals as possible, the author notes, "before these two camps become further entrenched as antagonistic, I would like to show how the two are each very effective and most effective when combined." This is a most helpful and insightful chapter.

A creative contribution of this book is Dr. Pita's integration of Erikson's Stages of Development with the processes, goals, and tasks of recovery from substance abuse. A very helpful chart is expanded upon through the last sections of the book. While the earliest stage involves the task of admitting lack of control over alcohol and drugs, latter items include giving up other obsessive-compulsive behaviors, identifying family of origin issues, choosing healthy new partners, and learning to take the perspective of another. These sections will be especially helpful to counselors and therapists who work with individuals in later stages of recovery. It will assist the helpers in developing a clear set of objectives for persons they are helping.

Addictions Counseling is a wise, flexible, and openminded guide that pulls together the contemporary knowledge about substance abuse into one source. Counselors just beginning their careers or those who often must do the work of counseling—such as ministers, teachers, and nurses—will greatly appreciate the value of this book as an introduction to the field. Experienced therapists will value the creative insights of the author and her skilled blending of approaches that many have considered antagonistic, such as the two views proposed by Alcoholics Anonymous and cognitive therapy. Finally, relatives or friends of people experiencing substance abuse disorders will find this to be not only an informative overview of the treatment process, but a statement of hope as well.

William Van Ornum, Ph.D.
Marist College
Poughkeepsie, New York

Introduction

This book offers expert advice on how to deal with drug or alcohol addiction and recovery. Whether you are a counselor, nurse, psychologist, psychiatrist, or employer, you can learn both the treatment and acceptance of this disease. If you feel angered and hurt by an individual who is suffering from an addiction, you can benefit from this book, which will help you separate the person from the disease. Until we stop angering ourselves and blaming addicted persons for their addiction, we do not have the emotional freedom needed to help them.

Before we accept our own powerlessness over the disease, as helping professionals, we try to control or cure it with the tools we use to "fix" people generally. A physician or psychiatrist may attempt to "cure" an addiction by prescribing an addictive drug. Some nurses have withheld pain medication from patients they know to be addicts. These nurses believe they are helping the patients by not "enabling" their disease; by controlling their disease for them. A psychologist may seek the "cure" in talking through the resolution of emotional conflicts rather than first stopping the addictive behavior. Some counselors in treatment centers have actually taken the patient home with them. Physically! I have been on a few "rescue missions" myself. This book can help you identify your own "cures" and help you understand why they are doomed to failure.

Being a recovered person does not save you from being emotionally disturbed by another's disease. Recovered counselors continue to relapse. Counselors will be actively using an addictive substance at the very moment they are confronting others on their substance use. Now that is the insanity of the disease. As

13

I continually remind my counselor interns, talking to others about recovery is not a substitute for your own recovery.

Irrational beliefs about the disease of addiction can get in the way of our effectiveness as helpers and in the way of the client's recovery. As long as the counselor is trying to "beat" the disease, he has not accepted his powerlessness over the disease. The issues for the recovered and nonrecovered counselor are different but equally confusing. This book helps the reader to begin to sort through the personal and professional issues that are involved.

After the patient or client has stopped engaging in the addictive behavior, what can we expect in terms of recovery? By presenting a picture of recovery across a three- to five-year time span, this book teaches you not only where the client is coming from but in which direction she needs to be guided for long-term recovery. People are often so worried that they will cause their employee, spouse, boss, or patient to relapse that they expect virtually nothing from them as long as they don't drink or use drugs. Such low expectations not only diminish the life of the person who is setting them but also prevent the recovering person from realizing his potential.

I wrote this book in the same way I teach my course in addictions counseling and in the same way I help my clients recover. First, I lay out the available concepts or tools so that the student or client can choose a way of structuring his experience of the disease. After the framework is set, I engage the person in the process of recovery counseling. My hope is that they (and you) will then take the building blocks and experience and develop an even better way.

Throughout this book, I have used both he and she in order to avoid any tendency toward exclusive language or the cumbersome use of he/she, his/hers, and so on.

1

The Counselor's Role in Recovery

Many counselors believe the counselor-client relationship to be the most important aspect of counseling. "Counseling is a process of establishing a cooperative relationship and then using that interpersonal interaction to help the client learn his or her desired appropriate behavior" (Hansen, Stevic, and Warner, 1977). Despite the fact that this phrase was written over ten years ago, the power of the counselor-client relationship continues to be the focus, as evidenced by the popularity of counselor training guides stressing relationship skills. For instance, Carkhuff's (1987) *The Art of Helping* is in its sixth edition and selling well.

In answering the question of how addictions counselors help clients get sober, we begin by asking how the counseling relationship differs from any other helping relationship. Each semester I ask my students to differentiate the various roles in recovery: counselor, sponsor, friend. This task is not easy because most of the students play all three roles and the boundaries among them blur. For your own survival, you need to recognize the difference between being a friend, a sponsor, and a counselor.

A friendship is a *mutual* relationship. The word mutual implies an equal exchange of self and support. The sponsor-sponsoree and counselor-client relationships are not mutual. Sponsors and, especially, counselors, do not ask their clients for help in solving their life problems. The sponsor has learned how to not drink or use drugs and, thus, can share this experience with his sponsoree. In sponsoring, there is no assumption of a level of education, training, professional ethics, or emotional well-being. The counselor, on the other hand, is perceived as possessing all of these qualities, and more.

The counseling relationship is a unique one. The counseling relationship is initiated and continues because the client feels a need for special help with a problem that she is not able to resolve on her own or through other relationships. The counseling relationship is structured in time and space. The relationship does not extend beyond the professional relationship or beyond the four walls of the office. The relationship is limited by time. The client typically sees the counselor once a week and does not have unlimited access to her through phone calls or social visits. The relationship is, however, closer and deeper than ordinary social friendships. Professional ethics and laws of confidentiality apply to this relationship.

Perhaps most important and unique is the fact that the counselor is there solely for the good of the client. The counselor's purpose for that hour-long session is to focus on the client and help the client get better. The counselor is being paid to do that; the client has no obligation, no responsibility for the emotional well-being of the counselor. Because the client does not owe the counselor anything (other than the fee), the client trusts that she has an objective listener. The counselor has no ulterior motive. Often, this is the only relationship the client has in which she does not place the other person's needs before her own. In the process of placing herself first and focusing on her own feelings and needs, the client gains a different perspective of herself in relation to another.

Counselor Qualities

There is surprisingly little dissension in the counseling field in defining the necessary counselor attributes. Even where two counseling approaches are diametrically opposed, they tend to agree on the qualities required of the counselor. There may be disagreement on whether the qualities are "necessary and sufficient" for change or whether they are necessary *but not* sufficient for change. The qualities themselves are, however, basically the same whether you are asking a behaviorist, a psychoanalyst, or a cognitive therapist.

Carl Rogers, who developed self-theory and the client-centered approach, has contributed a great deal to our knowledge of what he calls the "necessary and sufficient" conditions for therapeutic personality change. He points out that significant change does not occur except in a relationship. The necessary and sufficient conditions include psychological contact, counselor congruence, counselor empathic understanding, and counselor unconditional positive regard. Congruence refers to the counselor's being genuine or real. The counselor not only means what she says but her feelings also match what she is saying. Empathy involves seeing things through the client's eyes and being able to communicate this experience to the client so that the client knows the counselor understands her. A positive, accepting attitude on the part of the counselor means that she cares about the client as a person with potential. The counselor respects the client as an individual and is nonjudgmental.

One of the most valuable aspects of Rogers's work is that his theory has generated a great deal of research. Research findings support what we would expect to be true: an individual who can communicate warmth, genuineness, and accurate empathy is more effective in helping other people (Truax and Carkhuff, 1967). Based on his research, Carkhuff extended Rogers's theory into an eclectic approach to counseling. The term *eclectic* means an approach that is not tied to a single theory but, rather, combines selected aspects of various theories. In addition to the core conditions of empathy, positive regard, and genuineness, Carkhuff added concreteness, immediacy, and confrontation. Concreteness involves focusing the client's attention on specific behaviors as they are occurring in the relationship. Immediacy involves the counselor's communicating to the client what the counselor believes the client's behavior means (interpretation). Confrontation means presenting the client with her own behavior by pointing out a discrepancy in that behavior.

In *The Helping Interview* (1974), Alfred Benjamin provides added insight into this concept of unconditional positive regard: "We can best help him through behavior that demonstrates that we consider him responsible for himself, his actions, thoughts, and feelings, and that we believe in his capacity to use his own resources increasingly." No matter what the approach, all theorists stress the need for the client to feel that the counselor is concerned and able to help.

Role of Counselor in the Counseling Process

Part of our role as helpers, then, involves establishing a trusting and open relationship with the client. Whereas counselor qualities are pretty much the same across approaches, the role of the counselor in the counseling process is very different. The psychoanalysts and ego-analysts; the rational therapists (rational-emotive therapists such as Ellis, reality therapists such as Glasser); and the learning theorists and behavioral counselors believe that the counselor is some kind of expert to whom the client has come with a problem that she cannot resolve alone. This assumption leads to the belief that the counselor must take a more active or authoritative role in the counseling relationship. They see the counselor as being responsible for making a diagnosis of the problem and for presenting a treatment plan.

At the other end of the continuum of counseling approaches, Rogerians, Gestaltists, and Adlerians argue that because of people's inherent growth tendency or tendency toward self-actualization, the client has the capacity and the motivation to solve his own problem if provided with an accepting positive counseling relationship. Rogers, in advocating his client-centered approach, stresses that the counselor's presence or behavior in the counseling relationship does not directly influence the client's behavior. In the client-centered approach, it is considered very important that the client set the goals. Thus, the role of the counselor is to provide the conditions (e.g., unconditional positive regard); the client will then change on his own within those conditions. Rogers believes that diagnosing the problem and setting treatment goals create dependency needs in the client.

Rogers with his client-centered approach and Ellis with his rational-emotive therapy obviously disagree on the role of the counselor in the relationship. As Ellis states, "The rational therapist does not delude himself that these relationship-building and expressive-emotive methods are likely to really get to the core of the client's illogical thinking" (Ellis, 1962). Relationship techniques are viewed simply as preliminary techniques and, "the rational therapist goes beyond the point to make a forthright, unequivocal attack on the client's general and specific irrational ideas and to try and to induce him to adapt more rational ones in their place" (Ellis, 1972). Ellis places responsibility on the client; he views the client as having the capacity to change.

Counselor's Role in Recovery Counseling

Interestingly, a major point of departure between these approaches is a question of dependency. Ellis, through a didactic or teaching approach, clearly defined treatment objectives, and homework puts the responsibility on the client. Rogers, on the other hand, believes that client independence and responsibility can only be achieved by setting up the proper external conditions (empathy, positive regard) and then waiting for the client to change. The counseling approach of choice in addictions or recovery counseling would include both components as necessary and sufficient conditions. Recovery from addiction requires counselor qualities and the establishment of a therapeutic relationship as well as clear education, instruction, and a plan of action.

If a client suffering from an addiction comes to us and asks for our expert help in solving his life problems, just on ethical grounds alone, it seems, we need to provide him with an accurate assessment and treatment plan. As addictions counselors, we believe that while the individual is actively engaged in his chemical addiction, he has very little freedom of choice, that is what concepts such as "denial," "loss of control," and "disease" are about. If a cocaine addict comes to us for help and we do not confront him on his addiction problem, it doesn't matter how accepting and genuine we are, he is probably not going to conclude on his own that he must abstain from all drugs.

A major difference in treating the addictions is thus the necessary condition of an active, direct, didactic approach with a clear plan of action. This approach is necessary in the early stages of counseling: assessing the problem, helping the client see that the chemical is the problem, and helping him to stop using the substance. The approaches of Ellis and Rogers, although at the extremes, are not mutually exclusive. We need to understand that confrontation is a part of being genuine and honest. Understanding the complementarity of seemingly opposing concepts is the key to effective addictions treatment. The complementarity of concepts such as "Tough Love," "Responsibility and Freedom," and "Gaining control by letting go," are basic to understanding the recovery process. We give the clients the tools of sobriety and then we let go, encouraging them to use the tools in their own way.

As addictions counselors, we must be very clear in understanding the difference between accepting a person and accepting a behavior. This is essential to addictions counseling not only to ensure that we accept the client and treat the client effectively but also that we can teach the client to accept himself. We do not accept or pretend to accept the addict's bad (hurtful, self-destructive) behavior. The person, however, we accept as a human being worthy of help. We care about and respect the addicted individual enough to trust that, with psychoeducation and challenges to his unhealthy belief systems within the context of a trusting therapeutic relationship, he can become responsible for making his life what it can be. Later on in recovery, as the client moves out of denial and into a more self-exploratory phase, the conditions outlined by Carkhuff in his eclectic approach, or any other recognized approach for that matter, may prove necessary *and* sufficient in facilitating change.

In addition to bringing ourselves as human beings to the counseling relationship, what else is necessary for change? We must bring our expertise in treating addictions (a knowledge base and experience), we must bring our professional ethics, and we must bring our knowledge and skills in the techniques of counseling. The great distance between knowing how to get a person sober and getting the person to "hear" what we know when we speak, is closed by relationship attitudes and skills.

2

Choosing a Model of Addiction

Historically, the scientific community and laypersons have defined alcohol-related problems in their own way, depending on the political and social times, and their own personal feelings. How we conceptualize the disease influences how the disease is treated. When society viewed the alcoholic as morally weak, he was ostracized to skid row. Later, the alcoholic was thought to have a physical sickness and was treated by physicians in clinics and hospitals. Today, we are witnessing another shift as insurance companies become unwilling and unable to pay for the medical treatment of the alcoholic. The chemically dependent person is increasingly being treated on an outpatient basis more by counselors with the adjunct of Alcoholics Anonymous (A.A.) than by medical professionals. Such a shift is not unexpected or, perhaps, even unwarranted in many cases. The point is that the way we define and treat the disease of addiction is rarely determined by the scientific community as a response to some scientific truth. The way alcoholism is defined and treated is often more a function of what suits society's needs at the time rather than what is best for the alcoholic.

Why is it that our value judgments always enter into our concepts and treatment of addicted individuals? We are caught up in a moralistic debate about the addicted individual. We do not like to see people who lack self-control. What many angry people are saying is: "Why should they get away with their *bad* behavior when I have to be so *good*?" This ill-defined area of "loss of control" versus "willfulness" is the one with which we all struggle. Whether or not we believe the alcoholic willfully hurt himself and others or whether we believe that he suffers from a disease over which he has no control ought to be practically irrelevant to us as helpers. Our role is that of helper not judge

21

and jury. In this way, our position is similar to that of an attorney. A defense attorney does not refuse to represent his client when the client is guilty, that is not an attorney's judgment to make. Must we see every bad behavior as an accident or as an addiction over which the person has no control in order to help the person get better? Bad behavior does not make a bad person. We need to accept the person as a human being who is asking for help, even if he exhibited the bad behavior intentionally. We cannot teach our clients to accept themselves if we do not accept them.

Evolution of Models

Let me briefly describe the evolution of models so that you may begin to develop your own understanding of addiction. There are many models and I am going to discuss but a few. There is the moral model; the medical model including genetic, endocrinological, brain dysfunction, and biochemical theories; the psychological model including psychodynamic, learning, and personality theories; and the sociological model with its various theories.

MORAL MODEL

The moral model was the first model of alcoholism. Moral models emphasize personal choice as a cause of alcohol problems. Within the moral model, alcohol problems are viewed as willful violations of social rules. The alcoholic is viewed as having a choice of whether to drink or not drink alcohol. As pointed out by Hester and Miller (1989), in their book on alcoholism treatment approaches, this issue of personal responsibility for alcohol problems remains alive and unresolved. As recently as 1988, the United States Supreme Court decided that alcoholism was "willful misconduct" and not a "disease" beyond the person's control and responsibility. Again, I think we can see how the basis of this decision had more to do with what is most manageable for society versus what is optimal for the person with the disease.

TEMPERANCE MODEL

The temperance model was next to arrive on the scene. The temperance movement emphasized the moderate use of alcohol.

The cause of alcohol problems was the substance itself. Not until the temperance movement evolved into the Prohibition movement was alcohol banned. People began to rebel as the movement changed from one advocating the moderate use of alcohol to one forcing drinking control through moral and religious pressure. Prohibition did not end the selling and consumption of alcohol; it just pushed it underground in the form of speakeasies, rumrunners, illicit stills, bootleggers, and racketeers. Had the alcohol issue not been used for political gain, Prohibition would probably not have taken place. At any rate, for obvious reasons, the alcohol ban was unpopular and difficult to enforce. In 1933, alcohol again became legal.

Legalizing alcohol created a conceptual dilemma because most Americans believed that alcohol problems were caused by the nature of the substance itself. A solution to this dilemma came in the form of the American disease model of alcoholism. A major assumption of this model is that alcoholism is a progressive condition that is qualitatively different from social drinking. Alcoholics are different from nonalcoholics, causing them to be incapable of drinking in moderation.The central symptom of alcoholism is a loss of control over alcohol, the inability to stop drinking once a person has taken a drink. Although this disease could not be cured, it could be arrested through abstinence.

Moderate drinking was seen as impossible not for everyone, but only for alcoholics. This model was acceptable to social drinkers because they could then view drinking as morally right for them, because they were not alcoholics. This model was helpful to alcoholics because it removed the responsibility for the disease and justified humane treatment rather than punishment. The medical profession later accepted the idea of alcoholism as a disease requiring medical treatment.

CHARACTEROLOGICAL MODEL

Characterological models attribute the causes of alcoholism to personality disturbances. The assumption is that alcoholics are people with certain personality traits (such as oral dependency) and that the resolution of alcoholism requires a restructuring of the personality. The intervention under this model is psychotherapy aimed at resolving unconscious conflicts. In some ways this model overlaps with the Twelve Step programs. Those who believe in the Twelve Step program believe that recovery involves more than putting down the drink or drug; it involves personality or character change. This belief in the need also to change on the inside is evident in the Fourth Step, which asks the recovering person to take a moral inventory and look at his character defects. A difference between these two conceptions, in practice, is that the focus in A.A. is on stopping the active addiction first and then on internal change. Characterological models often view the addiction only as a symptom. The unwarranted belief is that the symptom will be removed as the person achieves a more mature level of functioning.

CONDITIONING MODEL

Conditioning models are based on the belief that problems with drinking are simply learned habits. People learn to drink because either the properties of the alcohol itself are rewarding, e.g., tension reduction and removal of inhibitions, or the behavior of drinking is reinforced, e.g., peer pressure. A number of different treatment strategies rely on classical conditioning (e.g., aversion therapy) in which the drinking of alcohol is punished or operant learning principles (e.g., community reinforcement approach) in which not drinking is rewarded.

A limitation of this conditioning model is that if it is just a matter of learned behavior then the behavior can be unlearned or relearned. From this conclusion follows attempts to teach the alcoholic to be a social drinker. After all, if it is just a bad habit, then the alcoholic can simply learn to drink more moderately. The problem is that the alcohol has already taken on a significance beyond that found in a social drinker. Were he just a social drinker, the alcohol would not have been worth the losses he has suffered. Logic suggests that the person is taking a risk in attempting to control alcohol intake. Another question raised by such assumptions has to do with drug use. For instance, we may ask: "Can a cocaine addict learn to use cocaine moderately?"

BIOLOGICAL MODEL

Biological models emerged in the 1970s. These models focus on genetic and physiological processes as causes of alcoholism. Some have stressed the importance of hereditary risk factors, whereas others suggest that there are unique biological conditions which predispose some individuals to alcoholism. A number of twin studies have shown a hereditary or genetic component to alcoholism (Bohman, 1978; Goodwin, 1976).

SOCIAL LEARNING MODEL

Social learning models are more comprehensive today than those in the past. These models focus on the interactions between the individual and the environment as determining drinking patterns. Alcohol abuse leading to psychological and physical dependence is learned, but factors other than reinforcement are taken into consideration. Social learning models now include factors such as people's beliefs and expectations about what alcohol will do for them. Thus, cognitive theories such as Ellis's rational-emotive theory of behavior would be included under social learning models.

Etiology

As far as the etiology (causes) of alcoholism, factors such as personality traits are not shown to be significant. However, factors such as prevalence of alcoholism in family background and cultural and family patterns around alcohol use are significant. Etiology and effect are often confused, as are the significance of etiological and maintenance factors in the treatment of the problem. We are less concerned with what causes addiction than we are with what maintains the addiction and how we can intervene in this maintenance pattern. Once a person has learned how to not drink, why does he return to drinking? Once a person has major negative consequences to his drinking behavior, why does he not stop and stay stopped? A dry drunk may not have had specific character traits prior to becoming alcoholic but he does now, even in the absence of the alcohol, because of the emotional and physical damage caused by the drug. Spiritual bankruptcy may not have caused the problem but it certainly helps maintain the problem.

Which model of addiction is most helpful for the treatment of the person? There are all types of alcoholics, problem drinkers, heavy drinkers, and social drinkers, but the people we see in treatment programs are not all that varied. They all have problems that result from their drinking/drugging and they have not been able to manage this problem on their own. We are not quite sure what the disease model describes or how accurately the description reflects reality. In the earlier A.A. literature, alcoholism was thought to be "like a disease." This view came from the often insidiously progressive course of alcoholism and from the frequent failure of will power alone to ensure successful treatment.

Today, much of the metaphorical meaning of the concept "disease" has been lost. We hear people say that the disease of alcoholism is "just like diabetes," but that is not accurate either. The amount of pain and suffering caused by an active alcoholic or drug addict is far greater than that caused by an active diabetic. In fact, the only way alcoholism is "just like a disease" of diabetes is that it has a physical component and it can be managed but not cured. Chemical addiction is not just a medical problem, it does not fit neatly into a medical model. We do not need to force addiction into a medical model to justify its humane treatment.

Despite the contradictions in the field, alcoholism is recognized and defined as a disease by the American Medical Association (AMA), and has been since 1956. The definition of alcoholism that is most often used is the one based on the definitions of Jellinek (1962), the World Health Organization (WHO), and the AMA. Alcoholism is defined as "a chronic, progressive, treatable disease in which a person has lost control over his or her drinking so that it is interfering with some vital area of his or her life such as family and friends and school or health."

Under this definition of alcoholism as a chronic disease, the following beliefs are held by the scientific community. Alcoholism has a predictable progression through early, middle, and late stages with warning signs at each stage. The loss of control over alcohol is primary to the disease and not a symptom of an underlying disorder. Alcoholism is permanent. Once someone has lost control over his drinking, he will not regain it. Alcoholism is terminal. Alcohol is directly or indirectly the cause of death for most alcoholics who do not seek treatment. Alcoholism is treatable. Abstinence is the necessary first step in the treatment of alcoholism.

The key concept and the one that defies definition is "loss of control." The concept of loss of control applies to the alcoholic's reaction after he has taken a drink of alcohol. This concept refers to the alcoholic's inability to predict what will happen once he takes a drink. A "sick" alcoholic or drug addict refers not only to the one that is drunk or high but also the one that is so consumed by the thoughts of having a drink that he cannot pursue happiness in self, family, friends, or career. This process of psychological dependence appears common to all addictions, be they chemical or object relational (loved ones). The person becomes so obsessed with the chemical or object that she is not free to enjoy life independent of this chemical or object, and outside help is needed to break this circle of dependence.

3

Phases and Categories of Addiction

There are no absolutes in the addictions field. There is no single pathway of addiction. The phases I present contain symptoms *generally* found within that phase but *not always* found in that phase. For example, the fact that some alcoholics never experience blackouts, does not mean that they are not alcoholics. There are various patterns of alcohol and drug dependence and these patterns change across the life span of an individual depending on internal and external stressors. There are alcohol- and drug-dependent individuals who do get sober on their own. There are others who get sober through self-help groups alone. And, then, there are the people we see in treatment.

Whereas it is true that some people do not need outside help to get and stay sober and that some people who had problems with alcohol in the past can drink today without obvious problems, those are not the people sitting across from us in our office. If our clients were like those other people, they would not be seeking help with their problem. So, even though it is true that not *all* chemical dependencies do follow the same phases of progression, those we come across in treatment typically do follow a definite pattern. The people we most often see do have the progressive disease of alcoholism, and learning the pathway of that disease helps us to see how far advanced the disease is and helps us to educate the alcoholic as to what he can expect in the future should he continue to drink.

You will find many definitions of alcoholism. One of the most useful definitions is offered in Jellinek (1962): "Alcoholism is a disease in which the person's use of alcohol continues despite problems it causes in any area of life." This same definition applies equally well to the other forms of addictive behavior. There are two essential criteria in this definition. First, the person continues to experience losses due to his or her use of the substance or behavior. Second, this use or behavior continues despite the increasing number of losses. A more formal list of criteria of psychoactive substance dependence can be found in the American Psychiatric Association's *Diagnostic and Statistical Manual of Mental Disorders*, Third Edition, Revised (1987).

Phases of Addiction

The signs and symptoms of alcohol addiction identified through research (e.g., Jellinek, 1962) can be found in numerous resource books (e.g., Kinney and Leaton, 1983). This research, which surveyed over 2,000 Alcoholics Anonymous members, found a definite pattern to the appearance of symptoms and progression of the disease in terms of increasing dysfunction. The following description of the four phases of chemical addiction are drawn, primarily, from Kinney and Leaton (1983).

PREALCOHOLIC PHASE

The *prealcoholic phase* is the initial phase, in which the use of alcohol/drugs is socially motivated. The person experiences psychological relief in the drinking situation and seeks out occasions where drinking will occur. A conscious connection is made between alcohol (drugs) and psychological relief. Drinking then becomes his means of dealing with stress. Despite these internal markers of alcoholism, the prealcoholic looks no different than the social drinker from the outside. This phase may last from several months to two plus years as the increase in tolerance to the chemical develops. The increase in tolerance is progressively built up to the point that it takes more and more alcohol and/or other drugs to get the same level of relief. Whereas initially three drinks might give a comfortable feeling of relief, eventually it will take seven or nine.

PRODROMAL PHASE

The *prodromal phase* warns or signals disease onset. A warning signal of this phase is blackouts (alcohol-induced memory loss). Other evidence that alcohol is no longer "just" a beverage but a "need" includes sneaking extra drinks before parties, gulping drinks, and feeling guilty about drinking. Consumption of alcohol is heavy but not necessarily conspicuous, but to look "okay" to the outside world requires effort. The addicted individual begins hiding alcohol and or drug consumption, camouflaging heavy drinking, and/or drugging in an effort to avoid facing negative consequences. There is an increased dependence on the chemical with more and more areas of life becoming associated with the use of the chemical.

CRUCIAL PHASE

The *crucial phase* includes the key symptom of loss of control. The alcoholic cannot control the amount yet he can control whether or not he will take a drink. With loss of control, his drinking is now obviously different from that of the social drinker. This requires explanation so rationalization begins and at the same time attempts to regain control. Rationalization is a type of denial, here the alcoholic is coming up with reasons or rational explanations for his drinking and drinking-related behaviors. The alcoholic will attempt to make external changes to control his drinking: periods of abstinence, change in type of alcohol, change in drinking pattern, geographical escape (moves), changes in job, and the like. All these attempts are doomed to failure and the alcoholic responds to this failure by feeling even worse about himself and angry at others.

The alcoholic is now beginning to recognize that there is something wrong, but he does not understand what is happening and begins to feel guilty. Drinking and/or drugging violates personal values. Blackouts increase as do the problems caused by these blackouts. The alcoholic's inability to stop drinking becomes apparent to an increasing number of other people. There is remorse caused by the inability to stop drinking but the person does not know what to do about it. There is a great need to prove to others that he is okay. As the person loses control of his life, there are more and more promises to do better. But the promises fail.

Losses continue to rise in all life areas: personal, social, financial, family, friends, legal. Drinking begins pushing everything else out of the person's life. Life is now alcohol-centered; family life and friendships deteriorate. The alcoholic begins to isolate.

Nutritional problems begin to develop because of poor eating habits. The first alcohol-related hospitalization is likely.

CHRONIC PHASE

The *chronic phase* begins with drinking starting earlier in the day and becoming intoxicated almost daily. The person needs a drink and/or drug to get going in the morning, and oftentimes tremors become noticeable. Alcohol/drugs reduce tremors and help the person to become functional. There is a loss of ordinary willpower. The ability to determine direction and control of life situations decreases. Drinking/drugging take its physical toll. The person feels physically ill most of the time. Health problems become obvious, and organ system disease develops. There is a sudden decrease in alcohol (drug) tolerance. Small quantities of alcohol will produce drunkenness. Drug tolerance suddenly increases with larger quantities needed to produce a high. The addicted person cannot handle the drugs as before and no longer gets relief or high, but cannot stop and stay stopped.

There is moral deterioration and the alcoholic can no longer maintain his value system. Binges become more common and interfere severely with maintaining a life-style. As feelings about self deteriorate, the addicted person always makes sure he is in the company of someone who is worse off than he is. Impaired thinking is evident in memory, problem-solving abilities, and psychomotor skills. Impaired thinking produces high levels of anxiety and panic. The alcoholic can no longer rationalize that his behavior is normal. Defeat is admitted as the person hits bottom.

Categories of Alcoholism

To complicate matters even further, in addition to alcoholics being found in different phases of alcoholism, there are also different types or categories of alcoholics (Kinney and Leaton, 1983). The type of alcoholic whose disease is progressive is called a Gamma alcoholic, which is the type just discussed. The Gamma alcoholic has a change in tolerance, withdrawal symptoms, loss of control, and progression from psychological to physical dependence. The Gamma alcoholic is referred to as the American alcoholic because this type is more common in the United States than in other countries.

Other types or categories of alcoholism have been identified. The Alpha alcoholic just has psychological dependence on alcohol with no loss of control. Relief drinking (drinking to cope, or not cope actually) leads to problems with family or work with no progression evident. We may call this type a problem drinker.

Another type of alcoholic found in cultures with widespread drinking and poor diet is the Beta alcoholic. The Beta alcoholic has various physical problems resulting from drinking such as cirrhosis or gastritis, but the individual is not psychologically or physically dependent on alcohol. Delta alcoholism is very similar to Gamma but without loss of control. The drinker can control his intake but cannot stop drinking for even a day without suffering withdrawal symptoms. Finally, there is Epsilon alcoholism, which is periodic alcoholism marked by binge drinking.

Since there are various types of alcoholics, and since some alcoholics do not need continued external help to manage their disease, clients in treatment often argue against a treatment plan that includes objectives such as continued self-help group attendance and total abstinence. I often use the following reasoning in response to such arguments: "You are in treatment so you are already not like those individuals who did not need treatment to stop. You are in America, not in another country, so chances are you are an American or Gamma alcoholic. Therefore, you can expect your disease to progress if you do not abstain from alcohol and other drugs."

Several questions routinely arise regarding progression and recovery. "Does the alcoholic/addict have to get to the final phase before he can get sober?" The answer to this question is "no." Everyone's bottom is different, and the bottom seems related to the person's value system. Some people will give up alcohol if threatened with the loss of their family, others will do so if they are threatened by loss of their job. Some addicts quit when they see themselves behaving in ways that are so contrary to their values that they can no longer stand it: prostituting themselves, for example.

A related question is always raised, "Does coercion work or does the person have to 'want' to give up the drug?" Coercion does work. Practically all addicted individuals enter treatment because they have been pushed by others to do so. The level of coercion varies but rarely does the addicted person willingly seek treatment with the goal of not ever having another drug or drink. Coercion works because it clears the mind and body of chemicals, allowing the person to begin to see what he is doing to himself. Often, given that time, the person no longer wants to continue on the self-destructive path. People who entered treatment because they were threatened with a loss of license (e.g., nurses and physicians) or other job loss appear to recover at no slower a rate than those who are not coerced into treatment.

A third common question is: "Is it true a person has to get sober for himself and not for anyone else?" I do not find this to be true. I think we do not really know what the person's motives are for getting sober. Parents of young children often say they only got sober for their children. A mother may say she is getting sober for her children but that is because she wants what is best for her children. So in that sense it is for her and for the children. Many women will say they are getting sober for someone else, at least initially, just because they feel they alone are not worth the time and effort.

A final question has to do with the relationship between chemical addiction and other addictions or dependencies such as food, sex, or gambling. Other than the chemically addictive aspect, the process of dependence and recovery appears essentially the same. The primary difference is that with some of these other addictions the goal is not abstinence but moderate use, for example with food and sex. Learning to moderate use as opposed to abstinence makes recovery somewhat different. By means of internal cues the individual must learn to distinguish use from abuse. For instance, a person addicted to food learns to distinguish between a feeling of hunger and a feeling of emotional emptiness. He then learns how to deal with the feeling of emptiness without filling it up by taking in a substance. We must always be aware that there is no known "cure" for this disease. There is no single pathway of addiction or recovery. We need to keep our minds open to possibilities we would otherwise miss.

4

Treatment Approaches

There are hundreds of psychotherapy and counseling approaches, but these approaches, in general, can be classified as one of three types: Psychoanalytic/ego-analytic, behavioral, or cognitive. One approach is not necessarily superior to another in the treatment of addiction. Rather, each approach has its place in recovery, and that place is determined by the client's stage of recovery and the specific treatment goal at hand.

Psychoanalytic/Ego-Analytic Approach

Psychoanalytic and ego-analytic approaches emerge from the theoretical base of psychoanalysis that was first proposed by Freud. Freud's psychoanalytic theory of personality is at the core of this form of therapy. As traditionally practiced, the therapeutic session is directed toward the patient's becoming aware of his unconscious motives and conflicts. Repressed conflicts and unconsciously stored frustrations have their roots in childhood and are the cause of psychological maladjustment. These conflicts can only be resolved when the individual becomes consciously aware of their existence.

Originally, Freud (1943) placed a great deal of emphasis on the release of emotional tension, a process known as *catharsis*. However, Freud soon discovered that it was not enough to have patients undergo catharsis; he recognized that they needed to develop insight, an understanding of the unconscious roots of their problems. Just as Freud discovered that catharsis was not sufficient, today's therapists are discovering insight is not sufficient but must also include behavioral and cognitive goals.

In contrast to the cognitive and behavioral therapies, insight or psychodynamic therapies tend to be less confrontational and direct. Psychodynamic approaches focus on past events rather than on present realities. They tend to take longer, and they tend to be geared toward a change in the whole personality structure versus a change in a single or group of behaviors or beliefs. The techniques of psychoanalytic therapy include free association, dreams, resistance, and transference.

In the early phases of addictions therapy, a nonconfrontive or indirect approach would not be as helpful as a more direct, confrontive approach in breaking through the client's denial regarding his addiction. Addiction counselors know from experience that unless the person stops using the substance he cannot get well. In psychoanalytic therapy, there is the tendency to view the addiction only as a symptom of an underlying conflict. As such, the therapist often attempts to first treat the conflict believing that once the conflict is resolved, the symptom (addiction) will be removed as well. Typically, this does not happen. The client must first stop the active addiction. If the client uses drugs to deal with his feelings, uncovering more painful feelings is not going to help the client stop using the chemical. In fact, the client will be more tempted to use the chemical as the bad feelings increase.

Neo-analysts or ego-counselors include theorists such as Adler, Horney, Jung, Rank, Sullivan, Fromm, and Erik Erikson. They are called neo-analysts because their theories are extensions of Freudian theory but with a greater emphasis on the ego. These theorists are known more for their theories than for their counseling techniques. The theoretical concepts provided by these theories add to our understanding of the whole person across the life span. Each theorist has something to offer the field of recovery. For instance, Jung identified a spiritual component of alcoholism over forty years ago.

When the client enters the third or fourth year of recovery, these approaches are as helpful for the recovering as the non-recovering client in working through family of origin dynamics and their continued impact on identity and intimacy in adulthood. John Bradshaw, a nationally known expert in the recovery field, is an excellent resource for learning about the place of psychodynamics in recovery.

Behavioral Approach

Behavior therapists tend to view alcohol abuse within a social-learning model, but they are concerned with the overt or observable behavior rather than with the belief and value systems of the cognitive approach. Behavioral therapy is the clinical application of the principles psychologists have discovered about how people learn. The basic idea is that a behavior can be learned, it can also be changed. One method of changing behavior is the learning and reinforcement of new behavior. Another method is the punishment of old behavior. Within this model, alcohol abuse is viewed as

> a socially acquired, learned behavior pattern maintained by numerous antecedent cues and consequent reinforcers that may be of psychological, sociological, or physiological nature. Such factors as reduction in anxiety, increased social recognition and peer approval, enhanced social ability, or the avoidance of physiological withdrawal symptoms may maintain substance abuse. (Miller, 1976)

Behaviorally based techniques in the addictions field have included aversion therapies designed to reduce or eliminate an individual's desire for alcohol. The most common types of aversion therapy are nausea, apnea, electric shock, and imagery. The goal is to reduce urges to drink, based on pairing of unpleasant stimuli or images with alcohol consumption. The results of aversion therapy over the long term have been questioned. Aversion therapy of this form is now used very rarely (Kinney and Leaton, 1983). Miller, a behavioral therapist himself, writes:

> Historically there have been many fads in the treatment of alcoholism. . . . Behavioral therapists have also been guilty of this faddism in the form of aversion therapy. There is a recent awareness on the part of behavior therapists that this rather naive approach to a complex clinical problem such as alcoholism is unwarranted.

A behavioral approach is most effective when a simple behavior needs to be changed as quickly as possible. For instance, sometimes clients say they are too afraid to attend A.A. In exploring this fear you discover that they are afraid to go to new places alone. The goal of A.A. attendance can most quickly be achieved by simply having the client attend A.A. with someone. You may set up a system for rewarding A.A. attendance to increase this behavior. After a few meetings, the client can usually go alone. If she continues to have a problem going alone, you may begin to identify the irrational beliefs that give rise to this anxiety and help the client challenge those beliefs. For example, the client may be saying to herself: "Oh my God, what if I say or do the wrong thing!" You teach the client how to challenge such perfectionistic beliefs.

Behavioral approaches are also critical in recovery for treatment planning and evaluating the success of treatment. This approach is essential because it is concrete, measurable. Either you drank or you did not drink. You do not need to rely on vague subjective answers to questions such as: "Do you feel A.A. helps you?" You look at the number of meetings the client is attending and if he is attending when he needs to versus when it is suggested by someone else. Every treatment objective you set up needs to be presented in behavioral or measurable terms.

Employing a behavioral approach helps reduce ambiguity about treatment goals. Behavioral or operational treatment objectives and goals also reduce the client's temptation to "con" the counselor into believing she is in recovery rather than actually working at being in recovery. Proof of motivation and commitment comes in the form of behavior. The client learns she will be held accountable for her behavior. The client must talk *and* walk the program.

The behavioral approach is not sufficient for dealing with the whole person in recovery. The view that alcoholism is just a learned behavior leads to the belief that this behavior can be relearned. The belief that the client can learn to control or moderate his drinking versus giving up his drinking follows from this assumption. This belief has led to a controversy between the medical and the social learning or behavioral approach, the "controlled drinking controversy" (Marlatt, 1983). If alcoholism is inevitably progressive, with a deteriorating course in *all* cases, then controlled drinking and self-control strategies are not only ineffective but unethical as well. In a review of the use of self-control strategies in the treatment of alcohol abuse, the authors concluded that overall effectiveness of self-control techniques has not been proven (Carey and Maisto, 1985).

Can an individual who has experienced long-term, alcohol-related problems but continues to drink become a social drinker, not just a controlled drinker but a social drinker who, by definition, can take it or leave it? The answer is probably not, by virtue of the fact that the individual is willing to put his life at risk in order to keep alcohol in his life and is willing to invest all that time and energy in learning and maintaining self-controlled drinking techniques. The idea of someone investing his time and energy learning to regain control over a substance whose reinforcing value is, partly, the feeling of loss of control (release of tension, inhibition) seems self-defeating.

We need to view the client as a whole person and treat every aspect of her being: cognitive, emotional/relational, and spiritual. Changing the behavior is a method for changing the way the person thinks and feels about herself, but it is not a sufficient method. We need to do more than help the client stop abusing the substance, be it alcohol/drugs or food. We need to help the client experience self-acceptance and satisfaction with her life without dependence on the substance.

Cognitive Therapy

There are many well-known cognitively oriented therapists including Aaron Beck, Eric Berne, Charlotte Buhler, George Kelly, Arnold Lazarus, E. Lakin Phillips, and Julian Rotter. The specific cognitive approach of interest here is that of Albert Ellis, whose RET approach is by far the most widely used and was also the one extended to the treatment of addictions. RET was originated by Ellis in 1955 and has become one of the most comprehensive, integrative, and popular schools of psychotherapy ever practiced. Originally a psychoanalyst, Ellis found that he could help clients overcome their disturbance through more direct, time- and cost-efficient means. Rather than passively listening to their free associations, Ellis began helping clients actively challenge and dispute their dysfunctional and irrational beliefs and to act against them.

RET became a cognitively and behaviorally oriented theory and practice, emphasizing active, direct, and systematic interventions in the here-and-now (the moment or immediate present). Whereas psychodynamic therapists focus primarily on past events and unconscious processes, and behavioral counselors focus on environmental contingencies, RET concentrates on people's *current* beliefs, attitudes, and self-statements as contributing to or "causing" and maintaining their emotional and behavioral disturbances. RET emphasizes individuals' innate capacity to change their thinking in order to live happy and productive lives.

The primary assumption is that people can change their feelings and behavior by changing their beliefs. According to the ABC Model of RET, negative life events we often confront are called Activating Events, or *A*s, and the emotions and behaviors that subsequently accompany these events are called the Consequences, or *C*s. People will claim that negative Activating Events in their lives (or in their pasts) actually cause their current distress. In contrast, RET holds that it is their thoughts and beliefs, or *B*s, about Activating Events that primarily and more directly cause their disturbances.

Let me illustrate this concept. If I surprised my class with a pop quiz, there would be various responses or *C*s. Some students would feel angry, others anxious, and still others happy. They would say they feel this way because of A, the surprise quiz. But we know it is not the A alone that causes these feelings because were it A, all of the students' feelings would be the same. What causes these various feelings are the students' *B*s or beliefs about A, the quiz. They feel anger if they believe I *should* not give a surprise quiz. They feel anxious if they believe they will fail or not do as well as they *should*. Feeling happy or excited would result from a belief that the student knows his stuff and has done well in the past on exams.

In addictions counseling, we are working at changing addictive thinking. Addictive thinking refers to the alcoholic or drug-abusing individuals' set of beliefs, self-statements, and/or attributions about: (a) their problem with alcohol and/or other drugs, (b) the many disturbed emotions that this problem causes and the disordered emotions produced in their attempts to change, and (c) beliefs and self-statements about themselves as people.

We teach the client how to dispute his own beliefs. Disputing is the process of challenging the irrational beliefs. For instance, the

A.A. slogan "Let go. Let God" challenges the irrational belief that we need to be in control of everything. "Progress not perfection" challenges the belief that we must do everything perfectly. We need to show the clients in a direct and personally meaningful way that their thoughts, feelings, and drinking or drug use behaviors are all connected. The clients are shown that they can stop their destructive behavior by challenging their irrational beliefs.

Which beliefs we are focusing on depends on the stage of recovery. Initially, alcoholics will experience emotional distress as a result of their strongly held self-defeating beliefs about their drinking itself or about being labeled an alcoholic. Later in therapy, these clients may also experience maladaptive emotions and irrational thoughts about the feelings of discomfort they experience as they make an effort to change. Finally, when alcoholics have stopped drinking and have overcome their dysfunctional thoughts regarding alcohol and their feelings about change, they can then focus on their irrational feelings about coping with everyday life.

Another rational approach to counseling which is well-known to addiction counselors, is William Glasser's (1965) reality therapy. As with RET, reality therapy, places a great deal of faith in clients' ability to resolve their difficulties through rational processes; on a present time versus past experience focus; and on the counselor as an active, confrontive individual in the counseling process. When an individual is experiencing difficulty, it is because she is behaving either irresponsibly (Glasser) or irrationally (Ellis). In either case the individual is viewed as having the capacity to change. In both approaches the counselor's role is seen as one of confronting the client with what he is doing and then teaching him to think and behave in a more appropriate fashion. To accomplish this the counselor may use a wide variety of techniques, which are spelled out simply and clearly in Ellis's work.

In the same way that Ellis would criticize behavioral strategies as palliative, I would suggest that for some issues and at some point in the client's recovery, RET methods are also limited. In late recovery, a more psychodynamic or emotional-healing approach is helpful. We have taught RET as a coping method for irrational feelings and we have challenged the client's belief that he must be perfect. But what do we do with feelings that are valid? We can teach a client not to respond irrationally to the fact that his parent was physically, emotionally, and/or sexually abusive, but we still need to process the pain resulting from that abuse in order to help the client heal. Without processing the effects of that abuse on the child and on the adult, the client often continues the same dynamic and brings it into his current and future relationships.

Group Treatment

Group therapy is said to be the treatment of choice for addicted individuals. I agree with this statement, based on my own experience and awareness of the dynamics involved in addiction and recovery. Group therapy works and it works especially well with alcoholics. Each of us operates as part of a group. The active addict's emotional connections with other people are damaged. "Isolated and isolating, rejecting and rejected, helpless and refusing help, alcoholics are oblivious to the fact that it is the drinking that has been causing the trouble. Making it in the world sober requires real human contacts" (Kinney and Leaton, 1983). Group therapy is an ideal setting for working on social relationships.

The group member brings his old experience into the group. His roles in the family of origin (victim, scapegoat, martyr), the way he manipulates others, his irresponsibility and irrational expectations, and denial of his strengths all become obvious when played out in the group. The group has permission to confront the group member on these behaviors in the "here and now" (i.e., as they are taking place at the moment) and, thus, these behaviors can less easily be denied. The group member learns about himself through his interactions with other group members. He comes to identify his feelings and his defenses. He develops positive feelings toward group members and confronts negative feelings as well.

In addition to knowledge about self, the group member feels a part of something greater than himself, often for the first time. He experiences what it feels like to be "a part of" without the fear of being rejected or losing his identity. The group as a whole provides a sense of strength, support, and safety as the members work together to change and to accept themselves.

In setting up group counseling for addicted individuals, the leader needs to consider several issues. What is the purpose of the group? What are the goals for the individual members? What are the requirements for group membership? Where will the group meet? How often and how long will the group meet and under what conditions will the group terminate? How will the group deal with an active member? The function of the group is closely tied to length of sobriety. Early sobriety groups would focus on learning how to function without alcohol/drugs. Later sobriety groups may focus on issues of intimacy. The longer the sobriety and the longer the group is together, the deeper are the issues that can safely be dealt with by the group. The focus of the group might be education, support, problem solving, socialization, self-awareness, or personality changes. Many specialized groups also exist today, such as groups for incest survivors, AIDS patients, and adult children of alcoholics, to name a few.

Running a group is no simple task. The leader's function or role in the group depends upon the purpose of the group. In an education or support group, the group leader's role may simply be didactic (educational). In a therapy group directed toward personality change, the group leader needs to know a great deal about group and personal dynamics. A support group requires far less education and experience than does a therapy group. We must always be aware of our areas and limits of competence in order that we do not end up hurting rather than helping. Yalom (1985) is a great resource for learning about group dynamics, from theory to practice.

5

Ethics for Professionals Working with Addicts

The addictions field, as a relatively new one, is just beginning to develop its own code of ethics. In their book on ethics, Bissell and Royce (1987) cover issues such as confidentiality and mandated reporting, finance and funding, competence, patient rights, exploitation of clients, and professional relations. They also include a code of ethics for addiction professionals. Although their book is directed toward addiction professionals, those whose primary function is that of counselor or therapist, addiction counselors are not the only ones affected by these issues. Many helpers (medical professionals, psychologists, social workers) need education about the disease of addiction and how to humanely manage the addicted patient or client.

Impaired Professionals

Impairment refers to objective change in a person's professional functioning. For example, work assignments are incomplete; conflict with colleagues has increased; clients, students, or families have registered complaints; or the amount of absenteeism and tardiness has increased. Often, the deterioration in work behavior is not publicly known. For example, in cases of impairment involving sexual abuse, this becomes known only when complaints by patients are reported to other professionals or to the state's ethics committees. Most fields are now willing to admit that a problem of impaired professionals does exist and they have developed a program for dealing with the impaired professional. This has occurred in medicine, dentistry, pharmacy, nursing, law, psychology, and psychiatry.

Firsthand descriptions of professional impairment related to chemical dependency, depression, or common life stresses such as divorce, loss of a loved one, chronic illness, and sexual abuse of the client are limited but available. One book with excellent self-report case examples is *Wounded Healers: Mental Health Workers' Experiences of Depression* (Rippere and Williams, 1985). Three books have been written by clients describing the relationships in some depth. Pope and Bouhoutsos (1986) present some common scenarios, and Gonsiorek (1987) and Schoener (1987) describe therapist characteristics.

What can we do about the type of impairment that leads to the sexual abuse of the patient? Largely, there is little we can do about the abuse of client by a counselor who has rationalized that abuse and finds it acceptable. I do not believe that education is going to stop such counselors and therapists because they believe they are the exception to the rule. For some reason it is okay for them, somehow they are helping not hurting the patient. Although a discussion of issues may not prevent the sexual abuse of a patient, we may become more vigilant toward this behavior in our colleagues and we may be more likely to believe our clients when they report such behavior. Moreover, although this extreme abuse may not be stopped, other more subtle forms of misused power by more benign therapists may be. We can recognize our own vulnerabilities, watch for the red flags, and take steps to keep the client-therapist boundaries in check.

Let us begin to look at the range of impairment. There are gender differences in the reporting of sexual abuse by counselors with primarily males as the perpetrators and females as the victims. I say "report" rather than commit the abuse because we really do not know for certain whether males are just less likely than females to report sexual abuse. It is more likely, however, that more male therapists sexually abuse their female clients than do female therapists with male patients. This is probably a reflection of our society. Women are generally more often viewed as sexual objects with men being portrayed as being dominant and controlling in sexual encounters. Sex is portrayed as a way for men to feel in control and to express their anger at women. Some male "therapists" even convince themselves that sex with a female client is therapeutic.

With regard to the female counselor and this problem, I know of many cases in which a female counselor became romantically and sexually involved with a male patient. A gender difference is operating here in that it seems more acceptable (to the counselor and her peers) for a female counselor to become romantically and sexually involved with a male patient than for a male counselor to become involved with a female patient. We are not sufficiently aware, as a society, of the fact that men, too, are emotionally and sexually victimized with the same consequences resulting as those for women.

What is wrong with this behavior? Everything. The counselor-client relationship is not a mutual one. The clients come to the helping professional because they are not coping well with life, they are addicted to something or someone, and they need help breaking away. They view the professional as having the power to "cure" them. They place their faith in the therapist and trust that the therapist will act in their best interest. The therapist is guiding the relationship and is in control of the relationship. The relationship becomes very important to the client. The therapist is supposed to be the healthy one and the client is supposed to be the sick one. Clients are paying us to use our professional knowledge and techniques to help them get better. To then betray that trust by using the client to satisfy one's own needs is obviously wrong. The patient will never view the sexual or romantic encounter in the same way the therapist does. There is very little difference between this type of sexual abuse and child sexual abuse because of the vulnerability of both to the adult authority. We cannot allow professional helpers to feed their egos by victimizing their clients and patients.

With regard to "love relationships," which are more common than you may imagine, the same reasoning applies. How can a sick person choose an intimate partner? This phenomenon of the patient's attachment to the helper always reminds me of Dr. Konrad Lorenz's imprinting experiments with geese. The goslings, upon being born, will dutifully follow any object regardless of how inappropriate that object is for their development. The goslings became imprinted or bonded to Dr. Lorenz. How can a counselor choose a sick person as a partner in a love relationship? There is no basis for mutuality, which is the essence of intimacy. If there is no intimacy, then why would the counselor choose the person? Simply stated, the patient will dutifully follow the counselor. The counselor is needed, she is in control, and she does not have to deal with the possibility of real intimacy, at least while the patient is sick.

Why do professional helpers who work with addicted individuals need their own code of ethics? There are unique features of the field of addictions that have to do both with the qualities of the client and the helper. A primary difference is that the field of addictions has, traditionally, attracted helpers who are recovered from the same illness as the one they are treating. And, where they are not themselves recovered from an addiction, the helpers tend to be people who are affected by the addictions of significant others. What is unique, then, is the overlap between the helper's own personal issues with those of the client. We must be more alert to boundary problems and professional co-dependence.

Co-Dependency in Professionals

Romantic and sexual involvement with clients, although not unique to helpers who work with addicted patients, does occur. I would include such involvement under the umbrella of professional co-dependency. Professional co-dependency, although we do not know how common it is across disciplines, must be quite common in the helping field simply by virtue of the fact that so many helping professionals in the addictions field grew up with the disease, either in the family or in themselves.

There are as many definitions of co-dependence as there are of alcoholism. Cermak (1986) makes the most progress in clarifying the concept of co-dependence. In his book on diagnosing and treating co-dependence, he defines it as follows: "Co-dependence is a recognizable pattern of personality traits, predictably found within most members of chemically dependent families, which are capable of creating sufficient dysfunction to warrant the diagnosis of Mixed Personality Disorders as outlined in DSM III." Cermak distinguishes "traits" from personality "disorders." Cermak concludes, "That while co-dependent traits may be widespread, the diagnosis of Co-Dependent Personality Disorder can only be made in the face of identifiable dysfunction resulting from excessive rigidity or intensity associated with these traits." His proposed criteria for the diagnosis of Co-Dependent Personality Disorder can be found in his book.

Professional co-dependency is just the extension of co-dependency to the helping relationship. Many co-dependent traits and survival behaviors are also valued clinical skills. Co-dependents have learned to put their feelings on the back burner, they have learned to stay calm in the midst of another's chaos and confusion. They have learned to ignore themselves and focus on the problems of others. Co-dependents are natural counselors.

Most addicts, in addition to being chemically dependent, are also co-dependent. Not only is the counselor then struggling with his own co-dependency, he is also helping a client who is struggling with his own co-dependency. The limitation that goes along with being a co-dependent counselor is that the co-dependent counselor has little awareness of self as separate from another and, therefore, has great difficulty setting up boundaries in relationships. The result of not having good boundaries causes the counselor to take on too much responsibility for the client's success in treatment. The counselor begins to work harder than the client because his feeling good about himself is dependent upon the client's doing well.

Co-dependency in relation to a loved one's active alcohol/drug addiction is often referred to as "enabling." The term *enabler* is used to describe the spouse, parent, child, or friend who encourages the substance abuser in subtle and usually unconscious ways. Ellis et al. (1988) describes three types of enablers. The first type is the "joiner," the type who openly supports the person's habit. The second type is the "silent sufferer." Silent sufferers do not make any attempts to change the substance abuser. Silent sufferers just take it. They absorb the pain and then collude in a conspiracy to deny the problem and to present an image to the world that all is well. The third type, and the type that sounds most descriptive of the professional co-dependent, is the "messiah."

The messiah states his opposition to the loved one's drinking or drug use and makes an open campaign to try and change him or her. In his attempt to help, the messiah usually intervenes for the addict in a way that prevents the addict from receiving the natural consequences of his drunkenness and loss of control.

The messiah "understands" the problems and wants to help make things better so he rescues the alcoholic or drug addict from the negative consequences of substance abuse.

Recognizing Our Own Co-Dependence

We know we are becoming co-dependent with our clients or patients when we are working harder than they are at their recovery. This is a big tip-off because it is the *result* of co-dependence. The counselor becomes overly invested in the client's recovery, and his ego becomes involved. If the client does well, the counselor feels well. If the client does poorly, the counselor feels poorly, depressed, angry, even hurt. The less active the client in his recovery, the more active is the counselor. The counselor is having feelings *for* the client and the client becomes more and more emotionally detached from the process of his own recovery.

Do not forget that there are two people in the helping relationship and the addict has lived his life with co-dependents. The addict's goal was not to take responsibility for the addiction by involving someone else in "curing" him and then reacting against this control. The client is not responsible for setting limits in the relationship. We are. In not recognizing co-dependency, in not insisting that the client take responsibility for following through, we are enabling the client. Although it may not look like we are enabling the client because we are expressing an inordinate amount of anger toward him, we are. If we are overly emotionally involved, then the client recognizes this and the old, familiar game plays on.

A more subtle form of professional co-dependence consists of our taking all the responsibility for treatment effectiveness and for taking treatment success and failure personally. Because our genuine role as helper does overlap with the "messiah" we need to be especially cautious about falling into the enabler trap. We do oppose and try to change the client's alcohol and drug use, and because of that we must also place responsibility on the patient for his recovery and whatever slips and relapses he has. There are actually many types of players within the "messiah" role. The common factor is that they all set out to change the behavior and then they inadvertently prevent the exact change in behavior they seek by not allowing the client to feel the negative consequences of his behavior.

New counselors often fall into the trap of "helping the client out" with all sorts of things from cigarettes to large amounts of money. The counselors look like they are being taken advantage of (and they are), but they defend themselves as just "being nice," "being there for him," and so on. The counselor is taking the client places, buying him things, spending his free time with the client. Usually, this does not pay off because the client must take responsibility for his recovery. The client must work at it and this is not easy. He must experience the losses that have come with his drug use. If we keep picking the client up, how is he going to learn to pick himself up? How can the client build self-esteem and self-confidence if he is dependent on someone else for his recovery?

If we pay attention to the balance of the relationship, then we can detect the messiah in ourselves. Where possible, the client needs to do things for himself. He needs to make the phone calls, search for a job, and get himself to a meeting when he needs a meeting. Are we doing things for the client that he could do for himself to "make it easier" for him? The written treatment plan is extremely helpful in keeping the balance. The client must follow through with the goals and objectives on a weekly basis. Helping the client means not letting him off the hook when he fails to follow through.

Another sign that the counselor is playing the messiah role is his accepting the client's verbal abuse. Why would it be helpful to the client to allow him to swear or yell at you? This may be typical for an angry teenager but the goal is growth not regression. If you tolerate verbal abuse from your client because your client "needs" you, you may have learned from your parents that the only thing you are good for is to be a dumping ground for other people's anger. The client must learn how to take responsibility for his feelings and the handling of his feelings.

Just because you are not playing a "nice guy" role does not mean you are not co-dependent. You can play the "bad guy," the punisher, and still qualify for the role. One type or variant of co-dependence is the persecutor, according to Cermak (1986). The persecutor is the opposite of the martyr. Persecutors have a lot of rage and they manipulate others with anger and guilt. A persecutor-type of counselor may attempt to control the client through anger and guilt. Why would a counselor yell at a patient? The counselor is co-dependent. If you are yelling at your patient, you need Al-Anon. You are trying to control the disease and the behavior of another and you are angry at the client because you are unable to do that. The battle has nothing to do with the client who happens to be sitting in the middle between you and your unresolved conflict. The client is a bystander in his own recovery.

The counselor's internal cues provide important clues that her co-dependence is active. Pay attention to your feelings. Does a particular patient bring up guilt feelings in you? Does this patient get you to do things for her that you do not do for other patients? Do you tell this patient things you do not tell others? Does a particular patient call you often with a crisis situation? Do you wish that this patient would not show up for an appointment? Do what we call "needy" patients always seem to be invading your space, making it more difficult than ever to maintain the proper boundaries and roles? What type of patient pushes your buttons? Do you work better with men than with women? With younger patients than with older ones? Be aware of your prejudices (ethnic, religious, gender, sexual preference) for they limit the quality of care that you can give a client.

Your feelings about your patients tell you a lot about yourself and about your patients. If you are "taking the patient home with you" emotionally, ask yourself what it is about this patient that causes that to happen. You probably need to increase the structure or limit your interactions with this client. Cut down on the client's phone calls as a goal of reducing the client's dependency on you. Limit your answers about personal information to ensure that the client is using the session to focus on himself and not on you. If you are "taking your patient home with you" physically, you need to seek counsel.

A final "red flag" to active co-dependence is taking over the management of the client's life medically, psychologically, and legally. This occurs with medical professionals. For example, a nurse may take the total care of the addicted individual into her own hands, and act against the advice of the physician in charge because she "knows" what is best for the patient. The nurse may decide the patient has too much pain medication and then holds back on that medication in order to "help" the addict not get hooked on the drug. She is attempting to control the patient's addiction and is inadvertently punishing the addict at the same time.

Some co-dependent medical professionals are of the persecutor type. Such physicians and nurses may respond less quickly to the "drunk" who needs help than to the person next to him. They are punishing the active alcoholic. The type of enabler (messiah, persecutor) does not appear to be determined by whether or not the professional helper is suffering from the disease of addiction himself. Helping professionals who are active alcoholics and those who are "recovered" are just as likely to be punishers as helpers who do not have an addiction. Apparently, persecutors have not dealt with their own rage and shame about the disease and they take it out on the alcoholic who is "out of control." The disease they rage against may be their own or it may be that of a loved one (parent, spouse). The bed-ridden patient is an easy target for these unresolved feelings about the disease of addiction.

One physician in a treatment center for addictions refused to give a woman patient a hot water bottle because the physician said he would be "enabling" her. Physicians can be "co-conspirators" to use Cermak's term, in handing out all the medication a patient wants regardless of whether it is needed. Or, alternatively, the physician can be the persecutor in not prescribing needed medication because he has a "gut feeling" the patient is an addict. We need to recognize the difference between compassion and enabling. We need not to use the "enabling" concept as an excuse for punishing people we perceive as being bad.

Some helpers in the addictions field either tell lies for their patients (to licensing boards, lawyers, family members, and police) or recommend that their patients lie. How much responsibility are you willing to take? How much control over the lives of your patients do you want to handle? Heed the A.A. slogans: Let it go, turn it over, we are not that powerful, we are not the patient's higher power. Every time you deceive someone on behalf of your patient, you are doing your client a disservice. You are telling your patient that it is okay to be dishonest, you are not showing faith in a higher power, you are taking moral responsibility for your patient. You are liable for the outcome.

This is also true with simple advice giving. After the patient learns how to not use the addictive substance, no one can tell him what is best for him. Only the patient knows what is best for him and he has got to discover that for himself, with your guidance.

Advantages and Disadvantages of Being a Recovered Counselor

Although I myself am not a recovered counselor, from my experience I can see several advantages to treating a disease from which one has recovered. Primarily, the clients feel so bad about themselves when they first enter treatment that they are more willing to talk openly with someone who is "like them" or "has been there." Some of my students who are recovered say that if, when they first entered treatment, their counselor was not recovered, they would not have talked to him. The counselor can serve as a role model for the recovering client; he gives the client hope by virtue of the fact that he is sober. The recovered counselor can come up with more practical solutions for day-to-day sober living than the nonrecovering counselor. The non-recovering counselor has to learn this information through her counseling experience and peer supervision.

There are also disadvantages to being a recovered counselor. As an A.A. member or sponsor, you help the recovering person by sharing your own story and the person in turn identifies with your story. A different process occurs in counseling where you typically go quickly beyond this sharing and identification format to focus on the client and his thoughts and feelings independent of yours. It is, however, very difficult for some counselors to switch roles or approaches, at least initially. They tend to focus too much on themselves rather than helping to develop the client's self, relying more heavily on the process of identification than on the process of empathy.

There is an important difference between empathy and identification. As Benjamin (1974), writes of this difference: "The empathic interviewer . . . tries to see the world through the latter's eyes as if that world were his own world. . . . Being there, he may be able to understand the interviewee; but it is only when he returns to himself, to his own life space, that he is able to help." In the process of identification, the client wishes to be just like the counselor. The counselor is asking the client to put himself in the counselor's shoes, to see things through the counselor's sober eyes. As Benjamin describes the client's view in this process, "I wish to erase myself and to substitute the self of the other." The loss of boundaries between the interviewee and interviewer is called identification rather than empathy. Loss of boundaries increases the client's dependency on the counselor and decreases the client's reliance on his own strengths and abilities.

The counselor's dependence on "her own story" in helping the patient get well has several effects. Personal information being shared by the counselor may be used by the client to avoid taking responsibility for himself. He may use the information as a reason to invalidate the counselor by reasoning, "She's as sick as I am. Why should I listen to her?" The client may spend the session taking the focus off himself and focusing on the counselor's issues. The client may become intrusive with the information he has and continue to follow up on it in future sessions. He may require more and more of the counselor's time and attention in order to continue a "special" relationship. He may begin attending the counselor's meetings.

If you feel your privacy is being invaded or you feel shame or guilt about the counseling relationship then chances are the boundaries are slipping away and you need to set them up again. You need to express verbally your observation of what you feel is happening in the relationship and then you need to set up new ground rules in which the responsibility and focus are on the client not on yourself. Generally, as the counselor's experience and confidence in their counseling abilities increases, sharing of personal information by the counselor decreases and, consequently, boundary problems occur less often.

Education and self-analysis of our feelings and thoughts about clients help prevent counselor impairment. Additionally, we need skilled supervision. Peer support groups are also very helpful in allowing us to express our feelings about our clients and our relationships with them. Keeping the focus on the client and maintaining structure in time (weekly sessions) and place (treatment setting) help to keep proper boundaries in this powerful nonmutual relationship.

6

Twelve Step Principles and Cognitive Therapy

Twelve Step Programs and Rational Recovery

For over seven years, I have treated the addictions by a combination of Twelve Step programs (Alcoholics Anonymous, Al-Anon, Narcotics Anonymous, and so on) and rational-emotive therapy. So, I was surprised to hear just last year that Rational Recovery (which has its roots in rational-emotive therapy), is being perceived not only as an alternative to A.A. but as critical of A.A. This feedback comes from my students who attended Rational Recovery (R.R.) groups in the Boston area. The students reported that much of the time was spent "A.A.-bashing" with angry expressions regarding the spiritual component of A.A. In response, A.A. members are spending time and energy bashing rational recovery, albeit outside of the A.A. meeting.

There is a basic difference between A.A. and R.R.; A.A. uses a spiritual component, R.R. does not. A.A. is based on the Twelve Steps, as reprinted in Appendix A. "Rational Recovery is an alternative to A.A. that doesn't have anything to do with any kind of higher power or spiritual aspects of recovery. It uses RET in its self-help groups" (Albert Ellis, letter to the author, May 1991). As previously noted, rational-emotive therapy was begun by Ellis back in the 1950s. Over the years, Ellis came up with techniques for treating the addictions. In the 1970s he came out with a tape entitled "I'd Quit but . . . Dealing with Addictions" and, in 1988, he co-authored a very good counseling guide for treating the addictions with rational-emotive techniques. Although Ellis has always made clear that he is an atheist, only recently, as the R.R. movement became more vocal, did the God-factor become a point of conflict.

In comparing these two self-help group formats from an outsider's perspective, I believe there are "human factors" which need to be taken into account: 1. The difference between a philosophy in the abstract or ideal sense and the way that the philosophy is actually put into practice by human beings, and 2. The tendency to misinterpret or misrepresent the other group's philosophy. On the first issue, let me say, that both R.R. and A.A. are practiced very differently from their stated purposes and principles. For instance, R.R. groups are reported to be disorganized and to spend the greatest portion of time putting down the A.A. program. A.A. members are no more likely to always live the Twelve Step Principles than are churchgoers likely to always live Christian lives. What I find, generally, is that group members take what they need and leave the rest.

The second issue, and the more emotionally-charged one, is the misinterpretation of program philosophy. Jack Trimpey (1990), director of Rational Recovery Systems, in my opinion, misinterprets the A.A. philosophy. He says that in coming to A.A. millions of alcoholics and other substance abusers learn that "they are wrong in what they think and believe, in the ways they act, and in how they perceive themselves. They learn to their chagrin, that they are wrong about the very meaning of life and about the contents of the universe itself." My first reaction to this criticism is to recognize it as precisely the same as that voiced over the years against the RET approach. RET, and, thus, R.R. teaches the person a new philosophy of life. In fact, I know of no other system of therapy that more aggressively attacks and changes people's faulty belief systems. The goal of changing the belief systems is to change the person's feelings and behaviors. If anything, A.A. would seem to be less aggressive in their attempts to change the individual. The individual in A.A. listens and chooses a pathway. In RET and R.R., people are directed toward changing beliefs, feelings, and behavior. Trimpey fails to see the similarities between R.R. and A.A. philosophies.

The difference between A.A. and R.R. is the spiritual component. Trimpey (1990) writes about A.A.'s message to addicts:

"For example, a substance abuser who decides, 'I want to beat this thing; I really think I can do it,' is urged to think instead, 'I can't do it myself. I am powerless over my addiction.'" A.A. does not say that the person is powerless over his addiction, A.A. says the person is powerless over alcohol. When the person is actively drinking alcohol, he loses control over the substance and over his life. Admitting his powerlessness over alcohol is the first step in his taking responsibility for his behavior. I do not think any aspect of recovery is more crucial to recovery than the person recognizing that he or she has lost control over alcohol.

Contrary to Trimpey's statements, R.R. is certainly advocating that the person has lost control over alcohol by virtue of the fact that the person is taught how not to drink. If the person really can gain control over alcohol, then why doesn't R.R. teach drinking in moderation? Now, that would be evidence of control over addiction! Moreover, we need to be careful about selectively quoting members, many of whom have their own hidden agendas or simply do not understand the principles of the program. If you have ever taught a class or counseled people, you know that people "hear" things that are never said. There is a saying in A.A. that speaks to this phenomenon: "You hear what you want to hear." I have clients who say that A.A. members force their religion on them. This may be true but it is certainly not the way A.A. was meant to be and it is certainly not the way most members or most meetings operate. If I believed that all R.R. groups were always run the way my students described them (from their perspective as A.A. members), I would never refer a client to them. It is always wise in the field of recovery to consider the source, not dismiss it, when weighing the information.

Let me make one final comment on this issue of self-reliance versus reliance on others. Trimpey (1990) states,

> There is no sponsor or buddy system in RR because these arrangements support the belief that one is personally powerless and must depend on something other than or greater than oneself in order to refuse alcohol or drugs. Instead of calling a sponsor in a time of temptation, members simply write down. . . . At the next meeting, the tempted one will have an opportunity to get group feedback. . . .

In response to this statement, I feel compelled to ask: What is the difference between choosing to call a sponsor for help and bringing one's problem back to the group for help? The member is dependent on the group. "Self-help group" is really a contradiction in terms. If it were self-help, then you would not have a group. If a sponsor is a form of dependency then so too is a self-help group and then so too are group therapists, individual counselors, mentors, and the like.

Is it really so important that we perceive ourselves as not wanting or needing help from others? A.A. does not teach its members to be dependent anymore than RET teaches people not to feel. Some people will use the philosophies in these ways but that is not the intent. A.A. did not make such people dependent and RET did not make them nonemotional; these people have found a way to fit a system into their preexisting perceptions of reality in order not to change. A.A. can help people get sober, it does not necessarily make people less dependent. For some, A.A. is the only "family" or social system they have. I do not think that a dependent person would be made less dependent through a short-term R.R. group.

Let us now turn to the real point of conflict between these two programs: the spiritual aspect. Treatment options are needed for the millions of active alcoholics; however, it is not clear whether active alcoholics do not use A.A. *because of* the spiritual component and whether offering a nonspiritual option will increase the number of recovered addicts. In 1978, Maultsby stated that "A.A. does not give any more effective treatment to alcoholics than health professionals give. That fact indicates that alcoholics prefer self-help treatment methods to those of traditional health professionals *but,* less than 20 percent of America's 20 + million alcoholics accept A.A.'s self-help treatment." In my opinion, the fact that 80 percent of America's alcoholics reject all forms of treatment, says more about the qualities of the disease (e.g., denial) than the qualities of treatment options. The active alcoholic does not believe alcohol is a problem, so why should he seek help for a problem that does not exist? If someone offered a treatment approach which allowed alcoholics to continue drinking alcohol, I have the feeling that the percentage of alcoholics in treatment would dramatically increase.

When it comes to the issue of self-control, we continue to get bogged down in semantics. Trimpey (1990) writes about R.R., "Members are helped to recognize that they certainly do have control over their actions and, in fact, have been in control of their substance abuse all along—in control, but making consistently bad decisions." This statement denies the power of unconscious processes and the power of physical addiction. The active alcoholic does not even know he is making a decision. He simply does not have a problem with booze. Does Trimpey really believe that that fifteen-year-old heroin addict in the projects is making a decision to shoot heroin into her veins? Did Kitty Dukakis, wife of the Governor of Massachusetts, make a decision to drink rubbing alcohol? If she were just choosing to drink alcohol, she would have grabbed a bottle off the top shelf. Does the drunk on the street decide to take a swig of whiskey to reduce tremors? How can you make a bad choice when you do not yet know you have a choice?

We do not have to crush one self-help program to justify the need for a second one. There are plenty of active addicts to go around. The more alternative forms of treatment available, the more likely are we to increase the percentage of recovering addicts. Ellis reports that there are now over 150 Rational Recovery self-help groups in the country. This fact supports the idea that an alternative self-help format is needed, although we might note that 150 self-help groups or, approximately 1500 members, represents a relatively small fraction of the 20 million alcoholics.

The success of R.R. groups in attracting a certain number of addicts does not prove one way or another that the spiritual component of recovery is nonessential. Alcoholics may be attracted to R.R. groups for other reasons. For instance, unlike A.A., R.R. groups are time-limited and, thus, the recovering alcoholic does not need to address emotionally the fact that he is suffering from a disease which he will need to attend to for the rest of his life.

R.R.'s success in attracting members does not speak to the issue of a spirituality in recovery. However, logically, we know that not everyone needs to believe in a God in order to live a healthy, satisfying life and not every recovering addict needs to believe in a higher power in order to have a quality recovery. As living proof of this logic are those happily recovered individuals who do not believe in a higher power.

From my experience, the most effective treatment is one that uses both philosophies of RET and the Twelve Step Principles through individual and group processes. Spirituality is a dimension of our being and recognizing that dimension furthers our experience of life. Obviously, if you do not believe in a spiritual aspect of self, then you are not going to focus on the development of that aspect. Aside from the spiritual aspect, both Twelve Step programs and RET are aimed at making philosophical changes in the individual. Twelve Step programs do this through a self-help format, and RET does this typically through individual and group counseling methods. Twelve Step programs focus on developing one's relationship with another, a higher power, and a group of recovering individuals. Rational-emotive therapy focuses on one's beliefs about alcohol/drugs, self, and others. Both Twelve Step programs and cognitive behavioral therapy have an essential behavioral component. In A.A., you hear about someone "Talking but not walking the program" and "Needing to do the legwork." Both approaches require some behavioral changes as proof of philosophical change.

Rational-emotive therapy urges us to accept our nonperfection as a reality; so do the Twelve Step programs. You can accept that you are not perfect without asking God to remove your imperfections. Accepting our limitations and then turning over our will are two different but complementary processes. From my experience as an addictions therapist, believing in a higher power further advances the client's recovery. If people turn their will over to God, does that mean that they give up responsibility for their lives? Of course not. It simply means they recognize that they will not always get what they want and that there is a greater plan of which they are a part. It means they do not always have to be in the driver's seat. On the other hand, from a nonspiritual perspective, you can learn to give up control over that which you recognize rationally you cannot control without believing there is a power greater than yourself in control of that element. For instance, you can stop blaming yourself for the death of your child without believing that "God has a plan and everything happens for a reason."

There are also some pros and cons to these approaches that have to do with what we know to be true of the disease of addiction and its treatment. When we put ourselves in the powerful position of deciding which approach would benefit which client, we run the risk of limiting the client's growth. For instance, some very intellectual and educated types are going to tell their counselors that they will not go to A.A. not because they do not believe in God but because: "I do not want to sit in a room full of drunks and listen to their drunkalogues all night." On the other hand, insisting to an alcoholic that he must attend A.A. or he will never get sober, when he has already stated that he will never go to A.A., is just as defeating of recovery.

Limiting self-help attendance to those groups which we personally believe in may short-circuit the recovery process. It may be that addiction is a disease where we do not know necessarily what the client is going to respond to, on a less than conscious level. We enter the same arena of risk here that we enter when we send physicians to Physicians Only Groups or nurses to Nurses Only Groups. These special groups for professionals may not cut through the denial that is evident in beliefs such as: "I am better than them. I have a different disease than they have. I am not that bad. I am not an addict. I can learn to drink socially." These faulty beliefs are not going to be changed solely through intellectualization. They are going to be changed experientially: Going to the meetings, sitting with "the drunks," and beginning to feel that he does share their disease. On the other hand, there are benefits to these special groups. The members can talk about how to deal with what are "occupational hazards" for the addict returning to the workplace; for instance, how to limit access to medication or how it feels to have such huge quantities of drugs available to them. I recommend to the recovering medical professionals with whom I work that they try both types of meetings.

A second danger of restricting treatment to a rational approach with a group of alcoholics and drug abusers is that, as anyone who works with addicts knows, there is a fine line between rationalization as a defense and rational thought as a treatment method. Addicted individuals are, by their nature, some of the world's greatest rationalizers, a.k.a. con artists. They have more reasons for drinking, for not quitting, for why drinking was not their fault, why it was not that bad, ad infinitum, than counselors can imagine. Getting them to *stop* being "in their heads," i.e., rationalizing, and to *start* feeling is *the* challenge.

Another potential danger inherent in using only R.R. is that the group ends after a limited period of time. People recover at different rates, for many it is a lifelong process. Will some alcoholics feel they have failed if they do not have sobriety by the end of the group meetings? Moreover, there is something positive and generational about the fact that A.A. has been around for sixty years and continues to grow and will always be there if you need it. People form lifelong friendships in A.A. and they go on to help others get sober as part of their recovery. We must always remember, however, that what works "works." A.A. is not for everyone, nor is Rational Recovery. We need to try out different approaches to see what works best for the individual client.

Alcoholics Anonymous also has its drawbacks when it is utilized as the sole approach to recovery. In particular, some of the A.A. slogans begin to be misused by some within the Fellowship. The belief "Let go. Let God" can become an excuse to not move forward and work to achieve what one wants and needs in life. The belief that "this is a selfish program" is sometimes used in later recovery as an excuse for not developing mutual relationships. There is also this belief that "civilians" (nonaddicts) do not understand "us" and, therefore, they limit their socialization to only those in A.A. and develop a sense of mistrust for "outsiders." There is also the tendency for the program to become "my life" versus becoming "a part of my life." A.A. becomes a place to hide out from life. Such rigid and self-limiting beliefs make for a very narrow experience of humankind.

Based on my experience, the usefulness of self-help groups has to do with the qualities of the recovering person. Some "high bottom addicts"—those who have not had a lot of losses, probably younger, better educated, briefer addiction history—may be able to use R.R. just as effectively as A.A. On the other hand, I find it difficult to believe that some of the low-bottom addicts, especially those with cognitive damage, will be able to get sober and maintain their sobriety using a cognitively-based, didactic, short-term group. In my private practice, I have found this to be the case. The older, late-stage alcoholic is less able to use RET than is the younger, early-stage alcoholic. R.R. may be more helpful with types of nonchemical addiction in which the goal is moderate use (e.g., food, sex) than with addictions requiring abstinence (e.g., chemicals or gambling).

A.A. has organized itself over the course of sixty years; R.R.

self-help groups are only in their beginning phase of development. As they develop, the boundaries within the group will become clearer. With such boundaries, the degree of disturbances, such as disgruntled ex-A.A. members expressing their anger at A.A., will lessen. Rational recovery groups will not be perceived as a forum for A.A.-bashers and, thus, will not attract them. In time, the antagonism between the two self-help groups will lessen just as it has between A.A. and Al-Anon. Rational Recovery appears to be a viable option for those individuals who wish to get sober but, for whatever reason, do not seem to get anything out of the A.A. self-help group.

Integration

Since both A.A. and cognitive therapy are optimal for different aspects of the self, the real question is how to integrate the two approaches. The recovering person ideally is always working on three aspects of self: cognitive, spiritual, and emotional/relational. The focus shifts from one aspect to another, depending on where the person is in recovery.

The client works on challenging an irrational belief system primarily by learning cognitive techniques in counseling, but he also learns to develop rational self-help statements in Twelve Step programs. The client works on his spiritual self primarily in A.A., but also shares this with his counselor at times. The emotional aspect has to do with feelings about self and others. I refer to this as the relational aspect because it is dealt with primarily in the client's relationship with his counselor.

The point of intersection of these two approaches can be seen in A.A. slogans such as "One day at a time," "Keep it simple." Both cognitive behavioral therapy, in particular RET, and Twelve Step programs stress philosophical changes, supported by various self-instructional slogans.

This points up the important connection between changing patterns of automatic thoughts and more general beliefs and successful recovery from addiction. "What alcoholics and other addicts tell themselves about their problem, the feeling they experience in trying to deal with their problem, and, most importantly, what they tell themselves about themselves for having their problem are the key beliefs that RET aims at helping clients change" (Ellis, McInerney, DiGiuseppe, and Yeager, 1988). The same can be said for Twelve Step programs.

Cognitive behavioral techniques are very important in changing a person's irrational belief system. For instance, there are irrational beliefs that are specific to drinking/drugging, such as: "I *must* have a drink if I feel badly." "I cannot stand feeling angry!" "Drinking will make me feel better." Then there are some more general irrational beliefs we need to work on with the client later in recovery: beliefs and expectations that the client has of himself and others. For instance, the client's demanding that others love and care for him: "You are my mother and therefore you *must* love and accept me!" Cognitive behavioral techniques are very effective in changing such beliefs.

What, then, are Twelve Step programs for? The Twelve Steps are a philosophy of life, the whole of it. Cognitive behavioral techniques can help get rid of, or reduce, feelings of self-loathing, guilt, anger, and shame, but it really does not tell one how to work through the valid feelings of anger, sadness, and hurt. For instance, clients can come to accept that their mothers did not love them and not feel a burning rage about that, but they are still left with the very legitimate feelings of sadness and hurt. Clients learn how to deal with their feelings about selves and loved ones through a relationship with another: a higher power, and a counselor who provides a sense of safety and guidance.

Books on counseling the recovering person tell us about the techniques and tasks used in helping some get and stay sober but they do not tell us a whole lot about the relational or relationship aspects. The client needs to recognize the strengths he has and develop those he does not have, strengths such as trust or faith in himself and others. Often we are not doing rehabilitation, we are doing habilitation. We are aiding in the development of a person, not simply stopping an addictive behavior.

Cognitive behavioral techniques are not complete in this sense because they speak to the cognitive aspect of the person, primarily. If A.A. provides an introduction and forum for having a relationship with a higher power, then the counseling relationship provides a forum for having a relationship with self and others.

In both Twelve Step programs and the developmental cognitive behavioral approach I use, the recovering person focuses first on self in admitting powerlessness. He then focuses on self in relation to a higher power and then on self in relation to others. In terms of his belief system, the client first challenges his irrational beliefs specific to alcohol and drug-related behavior, then his beliefs in relation to himself, and finally his beliefs in relation to others. Practically all of these beliefs have to do with the issue of control and power.

Twelve Step Tradition and Cognitive Counseling

The Twelve Steps are now used as a foundation in other self-help programs (Overeaters Anonymous, Gamblers Anonymous, Co-dependence Anonymous, Sex and Love Addicts Anonymous, to name a few). The Steps, as used in A.A., are listed in Appendix A. The substance or behavior is simply changed to fit the type of self-help meeting. The first three steps are all about admitting and accepting powerlessness. These steps are stated as follows: "We admitted we were powerless over alcohol—that our lives had become unmanageable." "Came to believe that a Power greater than ourselves could restore us to sanity." "Made a decision to turn our will and our lives over to the care of God *as we understood Him.*"

The next four steps are all about admitting and accepting one's imperfection as a human being: "Made a searching and fearless moral inventory of ourselves." "Admitted to God, to ourselves, and to another human being the exact nature of our wrongs." "Were entirely ready to have God remove all these defects of character." "Humbly asked Him to remove our short-comings." Steps Eight through Ten talk about making mistakes in relation to others and making amends for that harm. These steps state: "Made a list of all persons we had harmed, and became willing to make amends to them all." "Made direct amends to such people wherever possible. . . ." "Continued to take personal inventory and when we were wrong promptly admitted it." Steps Eleven and Twelve deal with furthering one's relationship with God and then carrying His message to others in the program.

Step One involves admitting powerlessness. In counseling, I ask the client to complete a Step One exercise. In this exercise, the client makes a list of those behaviors that demonstrate his loss of control over drinking/drugging. The client must then list ways in which his drinking hurt his relationship with significant others. There are both cognitive and relational aspects to this exercise. Admitting that he lost control over his compulsive behavior will help break through the denial that he can return to the moderate use of the addictive substance. When people relapse, it is usually through that insidious belief that "Maybe I can have just one." Hopefully, the person has changed that irrational belief by continually convincing himself that he did lose control and when he did lose control, he lost. He lost himself, his friends, his family, his finances, and so on.

What is the relational aspect of this step? If the person is in counseling and not only attending A.A., then this step involves trusting one's counselor and having some faith that the counselor knows how to help you. Asking for help is an important step because it acknowledges that the addicted individual does not have to do it alone and it risks trusting another person to help and guide him in the right direction.

For a while, the relational aspect involves the counselor's doing some parenting type of work with his clients. We acknowledge their pain and we respond with empathy. We offer the unconditional acceptance they lack and we teach them self-acceptance. We respond positively as their sober days increase and we encourage them to seek out a support system in A.A. with a sponsor and new sober friends. And, eventually, we let go.

What is the spiritual aspect of this step? Admitting on an emotional level that she has no control over a substance is a big step. Admitting that she is vulnerable and needs help is a necessary step to recovery. The person must believe and feel on a gut level that she is powerless to this drug or behavior. This is contrary to all that went before: The "I don't need your help" attitude, the lack of vulnerability, the powerfulness and egocentricity. In my experience, very few clients refuse to *try* and ask a higher power for help, and the more they try to communicate with their higher power, the greater is their belief in a higher power.

Step Two involves Coming "to believe that a Power greater than ourselves. . . ." The fact is, if you work with recovering people, you find that they tend to operate in extremes. This makes sense, for isn't an addiction a philosophy of "You can't just have one—be it a drink, a cookie, or a gambling bet"? Their belief in their own power is extreme as well, more extreme than for the nonrecovering person. People in Twelve Step programs grew up believing they are powerful, and this is as true for the nonaddicted adult child as it is for the chemically addicted person. They believe that they *should* have the power to change all manner of things. They believe that they *should* be great achievers. They believe that they are responsible for the pain and the happiness of others.

Within a cognitive framework, Step Two involves the client's acknowledging that she does not run the universe, she cannot control all manner of things and she especially cannot control a behavior over which she has admittedly lost control—be it alcohol, drugs, gambling, food, or relationships. If the client gives up this illusion of control, which is making her "insane," she will, in fact, return to sanity.

The spiritual aspect adds to this understanding of the idea that there is something greater than oneself. There is someone or something out there who is going to lead the way, is going to help if the person gives up the illusion of power. The spiritual aspect involves having faith that someone knows better than they, what is good for them. This may not be a "someone," it may be a belief in, say, universality; it is a belief that there is some positive master plan or organizing principle to the universe.

The relational aspect, again, involves trust, hope, and faith in the relationship between the client and the counselor. From that basis, the client is able to move forward and risk developing friendships in A.A. The client learns that she does not have to isolate, that there are people out there with whom she can have friendships. We can argue that only if the client comes to trust in someone or something (counselor, higher power) can she give up the need to be in control of the universe.

Step Three involves actually turning one's will over to a higher power. I find that many clients do not turn their will over to a higher power. They say they turn their will over but then when things do not go their way, they quickly take it back, which means, of course, that they never really turned it over in the first place. Step Three is a long process. Most clients can turn over their will with regard to the use of chemicals but, as far as other aspects such as intimate relationships they have difficulty in trusting their high power.

The belief that "everything happens for a reason" is one the client hears in A.A., and it is also a cognitive self-statement. This self-statement is made to challenge the irrational belief that "I *must* get what I want when I want it!" Such childish demandingness leads to overwhelming irrational feelings of anger and hurt that, in turn, lead to a drink or a drug. The spiritual aspect of this slogan or cognitive self-statement is the implicit belief that everything happens for a reason *because* there is a power greater than oneself who knows what is best for him or her. Relationally, this step involves trust: Trusting that the counselor will help and not hurt, will accept and not reject (even having heard all her "terrible" secrets) and knowing that she is becoming trust*worthy* by staying sober.

The next four steps focus on the fact that people are not perfect. This is also an essential step in RET. Rational-emotive therapy teaches that we need to admit and accept that we are fallible human beings who are not perfect and who make mistakes. If we are not perfect, if we do make mistakes, that does not make us bad and worthless, it just makes us human. In the Twelve Steps, doing these four steps also involves going beyond challenging perfectionistic beliefs to admitting them to God, another person, and then being open to having them taken away by God.

Steps Eight and Nine expand the person's recovery by involving other human beings in the process. In these steps, the recovering person admits to those he has hurt that he is aware that he has hurt them and has feelings about that. This is called making amends.

The client is always working on the cognitive, spiritual, and emotional/relational aspects of self. After the first year, concerns shift from not drinking today to getting along with others in mutually satisfying relationships. The client is learning in A.A. the limits of her power, she is learning to have faith in a God, and she is learning to develop sober friendships and to utilize a mentor. In her counseling relationship the client is learning to risk trusting self and others through sharing feelings and secrets.

The client in the second year of recovery is also learning to accept the limitations of others. As the client turns toward relationships, the real struggle with feelings about self and trust in others begins. For those who have given up the control of chemicals must now recognize that they cannot control the behavior of others. They cannot make others love them. They cannot get their children or parents sober. They cannot make their spouses happy. In accepting these limitations of loved ones, they are painfully accepting their own limitations. No matter how perfect they are or, alternatively, how dysfunctional they are, they cannot control others' feelings and behaviors.

Clients who cannot (will not) let go of their perceived control over a loved one probably need to go back and work Step Three. At this point of frustration with love relationships, we often see relapse or a return to other obsessive-compulsive behaviors: food, sex, smoking. The person does not feel safe (trust) enough to give up control. These behaviors are clear signs that the clients need more work on their spiritual and relational selves.

In summary, in this chapter I have shown the strengths and weaknesses of the cognitive behavioral and Twelve Step program approaches to addictions. I have also suggested how the two systems overlap and complement each other and how they can be integrated to create the most effective treatment approach.

7

Recovery Counseling Overview

A Developmental Model as a Framework of Understanding

Most students of addictions counseling want to know what the counselor actually does to help the client give up the addictive substance or behavior. They are asking about the process and the techniques of addictions counseling. In attempting to organize this process of recovery for the students, using Erik Erikson's (1982) stages of psychosocial development (p. 73) as a framework, I have developed a model developmental treatment plan (pp. 73–76).

Most people in the field will accept that recovery, like addiction itself, is a process. Recovery therapy involves facilitating the patient's growth and development through the phases of recovery. A developmental conception of recovery is not new. The most well-known model of recovery is that of Gorski and Miller (1982). These authors developed a model describing a process of recovery from alcohol and drug addiction. They present "developmental periods" from pretreatment to maintenance.

So why do we need a new developmental model based on the work of Erik Erikson? The old models do not capture both the developmental process and tasks of recovery. Hopefully, the new model will communicate the essence of therapy with addicted individuals: both the developmental and psychosocial growth process and the content (concrete tasks and skill development) in such a way that the reader can become an effective addictions counselor by utilizing this information.

Erikson depicts not only the tasks of each stage but also the internal psychological crises and personal strengths of each stage. Each stage presents the client with an opportunity to move forward or the unfortunate possibility of moving backward. For instance, the resolution in early childhood of the autonomy versus shame and doubt crisis, if positively resolved, results in the emergence of the human strength of *will*, but if negatively resolved will result in *compulsion* and *impulsivity*.

The most important concept to understand is that addictions counseling involves more than knowing what tasks the client needs to complete in order to stop engaging in the addictive behavior. Recovery is a lifelong process, and the client needs to acquire not only the tools or skills to stop using the addictive substance or behavior but also the personal strengths necessary to remain stopped and to move on to a fulfilling life. At every step in the client's recovery we, as addictions counselors, have the potential to help the client develop another strength. In order to do that we need to view each step in the process both in the short term and long run. Not only must the client not drink "one day at a time" but he also needs to develop qualities of *hope, will, love* within the context of a recovery program.

A second concept inherent in Erikson's model is that humans need to positively resolve one stage before they can move on to the next stage. For instance, we need to positively resolve the stage of trust versus mistrust in order to move on to a positive resolution of the next stage of autonomy versus shame and doubt. The easiest way to grasp this concept is by considering the connection between identity and intimacy. Most people would agree that we need a sense of who we are (identity) before we can choose a partner with whom we are compatible (intimacy).

Developmental Process and Tasks of Recovery

Almost every treatment objective or assignment has two purposes: the obvious task of giving up the compulsion and the second goal of developing a strength or resolving a crisis. The following example illustrates this concept. Patients in treatment centers often complain about arbitrary rules. For instance, one patient was insisting that she did not have to go to exercise class on a particular day. There are two therapeutic bases for the rule that a patient needs to go to exercise class. The first is obvious: physical exercise is good for recovery because it burns calories, relieves stress, and gets us in touch with our physical selves.

But an equally important basis is the process of growth in recovery. The more the patient is willing to do such onerous tasks, the more motivated she is to sobriety. Not only that but it is in the process of seeing herself doing these disliked tasks that the patient begins to realize her willingness to do anything to stay sober. The developing belief is: "Sobriety must be important to me if I am willing to do this in spite of my not wanting to do it."

Moreover, the patient is learning that she is not an exception, she is not unique when it comes to the disease of addiction. She is learning that she suffers from the same disease as everyone else in the treatment facility. Finally, the patient needs to, perhaps for the first time in her life, have faith that someone knows what is best for her until she gets sober.

The Recovery Process in a Nutshell

We will get to the specifics, but let us first review some general guidelines regarding the stages and the process of recovery presented in the Model Treatment plan. The first five stages are specific to recovery; the last two refer to getting on with life while maintaining sobriety. When the client enters treatment, he may deny that the substance is *the problem*. He continues to blame the job, the wife, the kids. He then learns through education about the disease that alcohol/drugs are *the problem*.

The client may admit at this point that he is more dependent on the drug than he ought to be, but it takes a while before he *admits* that he is an alcoholic and even longer before he *accepts* that he is an alcoholic. Once he can accept that he lost control over his use then he can rid himself of some guilt over his alcohol-related behavior.

In time, the client can identify himself as alcoholic and identify with other recovering people (for example, through a self-help group). This further explains his behavior and facilitates the identity process. He then has other strengths available such as purpose and competence. The statement: "My first priority is staying sober and I can do that if I continue to listen and take suggestions," sums up the belief we, as counselors, are promoting.

These strengths then generalize to other areas: career, friends, and family. The client discovers he can socialize, do his job, and perform sexually while not under the influence of alcohol or drugs. These strengths are available for still further development of identity and intimacy.

Generally, when your client first enters counseling a negative resolution of the crises presented by Erikson is evident. The client is withdrawn, mistrustful, and filled with shame, doubt, guilt, feelings of being "less than" or inferior, identity confusion, and isolation. I will call this negative resolution and presence of negative characteristics a *state* versus a personality *trait* because most of this condition is *temporary* and a *result* (not a cause) of years of addiction.

Prioritizing Treatment Issues

One question I am asked time and time again in the course of teaching addictions counseling has to do with the timing of issues in treatment. Students want to know the order in which they should treat client issues. Most useful in this regard is Maslow's (1970) hierarchical theory of motivation. Maslow proposed that human desires (i.e., motives) are innately given and are arranged in an ascending hierarchy of priority or potency. The needs are, in order of their potency: (1) basic physiological needs; (2) safety needs; (3) belongingness and love needs; (4) self-esteem needs; and (5) self-actualization needs or the need for personal fulfillment. To Maslow's hierarchy of needs, we can add a simple parallel hierarchy of treatment issues: (1) detoxification; (2) abstinence; (3) belongingness and love, group identification; (4) self-acceptance in sobriety; and (5) personal fulfillment.

Underlying Maslow's scheme is the assumption that low-order needs must be at least somewhat satisfied before an individual can become aware of or motivated by higher-order needs. Gratification of needs lower in the hierarchy allows for awareness of and motivation by needs occurring higher in the hierarchy. What this suggests, for our purposes as counselors, is that we would not work on self-actualization while a person is starving to death and we do not work on self-acceptance or childhood issues while the person is in danger of killing themselves with alcohol and drugs. Applying this same theory, if a client focuses on issues that are not relevant to her need level, you can bet that she is in denial and resisting treatment.

Table 7-1

Erikson's Chart of Psychosocial Crises

Developmental stages		Crises
Young adulthood	VI	Intimacy versus isolation Love versus exclusivity
Adolescence	V	Identity versus identity confusion Fidelity versus repudiation
School age	IV	Industry versus inferiority Competence versus inertia
Play age	III	Initiative versus guilt Purpose versus inhibition
Early childhood	II	Autonomy versus shame, doubt Will versus compulsion
Infancy	I	Basic trust versus mistrust Hope versus withdrawal

Source: Erik H. Erikson, *The Life Cycle Completed* (New York: W. W. Norton & Company, 1982), 32–33.

* * *

Table 7-2

Doyle Pita's Recovery Treatment Plan

STAGE I: INITIATING TREATMENT

Process:	Psychosocial crisis:	Trust versus mistrust
	Potential strengths:	Hope and trust versus withdrawal
	Therapeutic process:	Asking for and accepting help

Task: Admitting: "I cannot control use of alcohol/drugs."

Goal: Agreement on treatment goal: stopping compulsion

Strengths needed to move on to next stage: Trust and hope

STAGE II: STOPPING THE COMPULSION

Process: Psychosocial crisis: Autonomy versus shame, doubt
          Potential strengths: Will versus compulsion
          Therapeutic process: "I am willing to try."
                                  "I trust you."

Tasks: Follow treatment plan
          Separating from active loved ones and friends
          Working on Step One: Admitting loss of control
          "I will not use drugs/alcohol."
          "I will attend individual and group therapy and A.A."
          "I will get a sponsor."

Goal: To stay sober one day at a time

Strengths needed to move on to next stage: Trust, hope, and will

STAGE III: WORKING AND PLAYING SOBER

Process: Psychosocial crisis: Initiative versus guilt
                                  Industry versus inferiority
          Potential strengths: Purpose versus inhibition
                                  Competence versus inertia
          Therapeutic process: "I admit that I have the disease."
                                  "My purpose is to stay sober."
                                  "I am a worthwhile person."

Tasks: Psychoeducation
          Working on first three steps
          Returning to work as a recovering person
          Learning to parent sober and nonco-dependently
          Learning to play, enjoy leisure time, relax, have fun

Goal: Learning to work and play sober

Strengths needed to move on to next stage: Trust, hope, will,
purpose, competence

STAGE IV: IDENTITY DEVELOPMENT SPECIFIC TO SOBRIETY

Process: Psychosocial crisis: Identity versus identity confusion
          Potential strengths: Fidelity versus repudiation
          Therapeutic process: Faith in recovery
                                  Faith in sober self
                                  Faith in higher power
                                  "I am trustworthy."
                                  "I am worthy of respect."

Tasks: Identify and challenge irrational beliefs about self
          Accepting: "I am a recovering alcoholic/addict."
          Learn to accept and care for self
          Work on self-esteem and express feelings about self
          Working Steps Two and Three

Goal: To admit and accept: "I am an alcoholic."
          To begin to identify a spiritual self

Strengths needed to move on to the next stage: Trust, hope, will,
purpose, competence, faith

STAGE V: INTIMACY DEVELOPMENT SPECIFIC TO SOBRIETY

Process: Psychosocial crisis: Intimacy (in friendships) versus
                                    isolation
          Potential strengths: Love (in sobriety) versus exclusivity
          Therapeutic process: Learning about relationships
                                    Honesty and trustworthiness
                                    Expressing feelings to others
                                    Taking risks
                                    Giving and getting needs met

Tasks: Working on relapse prevention
          Getting honest
          Joining a self-help group
          Joining a Step Group
          Expressing feelings in a therapy group
          Asking for something
          Learning assertion skills
          Making new sober friends
          Socializing with friends, family, relatives
          Recognizing and giving up co-dependent behaviors

Goal: To gain socialization and relationship skills

Strengths needed to move on to next stage: Trust, hope, will,
purpose, competence, faith, love

STAGE VI: IDENTITY DEVELOPMENT

Process: Psychosocial crisis: Identity versus identity confusion
          Potential strengths: Identity (sense of self) and fidelity
                                    versus repudiation
          Therapeutic process: Learning about self
                                    Self in relation to family of origin
                                    Self in relation to immediate family
                                    Relevance of roles to present
                                    identity

Tasks: Giving up other obsessive-compulsive behaviors: food,
             cigarettes, workaholism
          Identifying family of origin issues: alcoholism,
             sexual abuse, abandonment
          Identifying feelings about childhood issues
          Giving up old family role: scapegoat, mascot, hero
          Identifying career-related strengths and goals
          Furthering education, making career changes

Goals: To discover who I am now, my strengths and needs

Strengths needed to move on to next stage: Trust, hope, will,
purpose, competence, faith, love, identity

STAGE VII: INTIMACY IN LOVE RELATIONSHIPS

Process: Psychosocial crisis: Intimacy versus isolation
          Potential strengths: Mature love versus role-defined
                                    love
          Therapeutic process: Moving from egoistic to mature
                                    intimacy

Tasks: Preventing substitute addictions: smoking, eating, sex
          New view of current love relationships
          Giving up unhealthy love relationships
          Choosing healthy new partners
          Getting needs met and giving love
          Accepting partners
          Dealing with co-dependency with love partners
          Learning to take the perspective of another
          Learning to be less self-centered

Goal: To be able to love in a healthy mutually satisfying way

8

Stage I: Initiating Treatment

Stage I lasts from one day to three months and consists of the actively addicted individual's initiating treatment and agreeing to *try* to stop engaging in the addictive behavior. The primary goal for Stage I, then, is to break through the client's denial regarding his use of alcohol and drugs. The client or patient does not have to believe that he is an alcoholic in order to agree that he needs to do something about the role of the substance in his life. We only need to get the client to see that his drinking is a problem and causes problems for him. We can then pose the following question: "You agree that alcohol causes all these problems and yet you maintain that you do not *need* alcohol. So *if* alcohol is *not* that important to you, then why not give it up?"

We may share with the client our belief that he is an alcoholic, based on the concrete evidence before us and our experience as addictions specialists. However, we are not going to *demand* that the client admit that he is an alcoholic. Believing that one has a problem with alcohol is easier to accept at this point than is believing that one is an alcoholic—with all of the stigma that is attached to that label. If you begin fighting with your client, he probably will not listen to you because you do not yet have a therapeutic relationship. You will sound no different from that nagging spouse, friend, or parent who insists that he sees things her way.

Three Aspects of Self

As stated, the client and counselor are always working on all three aspects of self: emotional, spiritual, and cognitive. The relative dominance of one aspect over another varies depending on the point in recovery, the setting at the moment (A.A. or counselor's office), and the approach of the counselor (one will focus on the spiritual aspect early on and another will focus on the cognitive aspect). The goal is simply to get the client to agree to stop using, and the effectiveness of the approach at this point in recovery has a lot to do with what the client is willing to "hear."

Based on my experience, most clients who are just initiating treatment are doing so partly because they choose to and partly because they are pressured into it. These clients simply want the pain to stop and they want to get people off their backs. They do not necessarily believe that they need to give up alcohol and they do not necessarily believe in a God or a higher power. They do not even necessarily believe that there is life without alcohol/drugs.

Whether you are talking about inpatient or outpatient treatment, the focus is on the cognitive aspect of self: educating the client about the disease concept, teaching him how to identify his faulty beliefs about the role of alcohol and drugs in his life, helping the client explore his beliefs about what got him into treatment (e.g., spiritual or religious beliefs, personal responsibility, outside stressors) and, most importantly, showing him what he needs to do in order to feel better. You are helping the client to identify the beliefs he has and you are teaching him how to challenge those beliefs.

Some of those beliefs about alcohol that you challenge early in treatment include: "Alcohol is *not* a problem." "Alcohol/drugs are the *best* and *only* way to solve emotional problems." "I cannot stand not having a drink." A belief about self that you continue to challenge includes: "I am worthless because I am an alcoholic." More of these beliefs, as well as ways to challenge such beliefs, are offered by Ellis et al. (1988).

The primary cognitive component, however, has to do with the belief about trusting and not trusting, and this belief is developing within the context of the client-counselor relationship. So the client-counselor relationship is already important. The psychosocial crisis for Stage I is trust versus mistrust. The potential personal strengths to come out of this stage are *hope* and *trust*. The relational aspect involves the client's seeing that he needs help, asking for help, and accepting help. If the client is to accept these new beliefs regarding alcohol and drugs, then he must have some trust in the source: You.

We have previously discussed the personal qualities that contribute to the client's trusting the counselor: empathy, respect, care, and unconditional acceptance. You do not have to love your client or accept his behavior, you simply have to accept him as a human being and care about his getting better. If you batter your client with the label "alcoholic," "drug addict," or "drunk" before he even has a reason to care about what you are saying, then he is going to use his anger at your labels for a reason *not* to hear anything. If you are judgmental and beat down your client, he will not be able to get up and get sober. Remember, your client has been beaten by the best of them, including himself. You need to sound different from the others.

We need to offer the patient the "hope" that things will get better *if* he stops using addictive substances. We are saying in effect: "You can trust me. There is a way out for you and I can show it to you. Once I show you how to quit using and stay sober, you are going to have to make the commitment to follow through." Whether or not he believes you has to do with whether he perceives you as trustworthy and also how entrenched his denial system is. We are never wholly responsible for breaking through the denial system of another. But there is no question that we can facilitate the client's choice to give sobriety a shot. There is also no question that if we perceive our client as hopeless then he will gain no trust or hope from his relationship with us; he will simply feel more hopeless than ever.

The importance of the relational and spiritual aspects become more evident as the client progresses through his recovery. The relational and spiritual aspects impact on the very core of the recovering person. She begins to ask questions such as: "Am I an honest person? Am I trustworthy? Am I going to work on gaining the trust of others? Am I worthy of a loving spouse? Am I worthy as a parent?" Because one cannot escape either herself or her higher power, these aspects are crucial in the development of honesty. This personal quality of honesty is put to the test in sobriety again and again.

Stage I Tasks

Let us deal first with the typical case in Stage I. Typically, the client enters treatment believing that he needs help. He may not be willing to admit that alcohol is *the* problem but he is willing to admit that alcohol is *a* problem. In this case, usually the client simply agrees to the treatment plan within the first couple of sessions.

The primary task of Stage I is the development and signing of the treatment plan. The concrete proof of a contract between client and counselor is the treatment plan. In signing the treatment plan, the client is saying, in effect, "I admit that I have a problem and I need help. I am taking responsibility for getting the help I need." In the signing of the treatment plan by you and the client, the two of you are recognizing the beginnings of a therapeutic relationship. There is some degree of trust and commitment to a mutually agreed-upon plan of action.

The components of the treatment plan vary depending upon the individual case and the point at which the person is in recovery, but the common element is the client's statement that "I will try not to use alcohol and drugs." A sample treatment plan for Stage I for both inpatient and outpatient treatment can be found in Appendix B. From this sample plan, you can see that the client is agreeing to attend individual and group therapy and is agreeing to attend A.A. or another appropriate self-help group. She does not have to believe that she is an alcoholic to go to meetings. She may also be agreeing to make some changes with regard to work or family. In the typical case, the individual will agree to stop engaging in the addictive behavior but will continue to disagree with the specific methods of accomplishing this. For instance, she may disagree with the number of A.A. meetings or the goal of not becoming intimately involved with a new partner for the first year of sobriety.

The client progresses to Stage II when she admits to a loss of control over the substance and agrees to try to not use alcohol and drugs. In order to do so, the client has achieved some level of trust and hope regarding living without the use of drugs and alcohol. The length of Stage I depends on factors such as denial; length of drugging/drinking history; external motivators such as spouse, job, and children; and number of losses. This phase covers the period between the point at which the client initiated therapy with you and agrees to the treatment plan or, alternatively, drops out of treatment on her own or is referred elsewhere.

Clients may agree to try to stop using, but are doing so out of compliance not because they have positively resolved the Stage I crisis. Compliance sometimes results from the counselor's verbally beating up on the patient. The client will agree to try to stop drinking simply to get the counselor off his back. Compliance is a problem which does not become apparent until Stage II and, thus, is discussed there.

Resistance and Solutions in Stage I

It should come as no surprise to the reader that not all clients agree to try to stop drinking/drugging. What can you do if the client *refuses* to *try* to stop using addictive substances? The client is in denial and is maintaining denial despite your efforts. If the client refuses to try to stop and you are convinced that he must stop, there is little more you can do other than refer him elsewhere. You can employ several techniques in Stage I to attempt to break through the client's denial.

You may try an intervention, essentially repeating a step taken to get the client into treatment in the first place. You may bring in family, friends, physician, and employers to break through the client's denial that alcohol and drugs are a problem. Sometimes, once the client has entered treatment, you can gain the cooperation of loved ones who are now willing to come in and confront the client.

Use of Contracts. If you do not have any leverage, such as the threat of a job or family loss, you may try an "If-Then" contract. In this contract, the client attempts to prove to you that he is not an alcoholic by controlling his alcohol intake. The two of you set a limit as to what constitutes "social drinking." The contract between you and the client states: "*If* I go beyond my limit of (for example) two glasses of wine two times per week, *then* I will agree I do not have control over my drinking and I will try to stop drinking." If your assessment is correct and the client is an alcoholic then he will not be able to maintain this limit because, by definition, he has lost control over alcohol/drugs.

There are several circumstances in which the "If-Then" contract would not be recommended. One case involves a third party, and this third party has abstinence as a condition of its contract with you and the client, for instance, where there is a return-to-work agreement or a licensing board involved. A second case is one in which the client is bargaining with the use of illicit drugs. You cannot agree to the use of illegal drugs for ethical reasons. Another case would be the physically sick patient or the suicidal patient. The suicidal patient is especially risky, particularly when he is on medication. If a client is on medication and consuming alcohol, you may involve the prescribing physician in helping break through the denial.

The client may be in too much denial to make any kind of commitment to sobriety. At this point, the best thing we can do for the client is to admit that we cannot help him and to suggest that he needs some other form of treatment or that no treatment will help until he is willing to do something to help himself. We must not let our egos get in the way of our admitting our own powerlessness over the active alcoholic who refuses to ask for our help.

9

Stage II: Stopping the Compulsion

Stage II consists of the recovering individual's stopping the addictive behavior and staying stopped for at least a six-month period of time. The primary treatment goal is to provide the external and internal structure necessary to help the client not use the addictive substance or engage in the addictive behavior (such as gambling or sex addiction). At this very early stage of recovery, we help hold the client's environment stable so that the healing process may begin. The A.A. slogan "Keep it simple" is the one we need to heed. Establishing this external structure may take from three to six months.

The psychosocial crisis of Stage II is autonomy versus shame, doubt. The potential strength is will versus compulsion. The three aspects of self begin to emerge. In the context of the counseling relationship, the client is helped to look at his cognitive, spiritual, and emotional/relational self. In so doing, he begins to resolve the question of whether or not he is an alcoholic. The client is asked: "What are you willing to do to get sober?" As the feelings of shame and doubt emerge, we help the client see that he can get sober and sobriety is the only way to rid himself of shame and doubt.

In the counseling relationship, we are helping the client to see that there is only one alternative to living in this fear and to drinking: learning how to live a sober life. There is great indecision at this point between choosing to try to get sober and choosing to simply reactivate the compulsion. The client is asking himself: "Can I be autonomous and move forward to a positive life where I will be taking responsibility for getting my needs met in a healthy way?" Or, alternatively, "Will I remain dependent upon my addiction as a way of avoiding life? What if I fail? If I try and fail, then I will be a failure, a loser."

Three Aspects of Self

On the cognitive front, the client's beliefs about his ability to control his use of alcohol/drugs are challenged. They are challenged through cognitive techniques within the counseling relationship. The goal is for the client to admit his powerlessness over alcohol. Admitting powerlessness over alcohol opens up feelings of shame and doubt as the person sees he is vulnerable. He sees that it is the drug and not himself that has been in control of his life. But he must be willing to work at this self-awareness. The client learns the difference between willingness and willfulness. Willfulness is "doing it his way," "being in control." Willingness involves giving up enough control so that he is open to the suggestions and feedback of others. He is scared because he recognizes on an emotional level that if he has lost control over alcohol in the past, then he can lose control over alcohol again.

We continue to work with the client on the disease concept and loss of control, and how it relates to the client personally. This kind of personalized education is called psychoeducation. You begin to challenge the "badness" of being alcoholic. You challenge these misperceptions by asking questions such as: "What does it mean to be an alcoholic?" "What does an alcoholic look like?" "How do you know that you are an alcoholic?" The client needs to be convinced that having one drink is not worth the risk of losing something important. You continue to work on Step One, showing the client how his life has become unmanageable as a result of alcohol and drug use.

The spiritual aspect is emerging as a function of several things. The spiritual aspect becomes increasingly dominant as the client considers Step Two: "Came to believe that a Power greater than ourselves could restore us to sanity." The client is attending a Twelve Step program and is faced with the question of a higher power every time he goes, if he is listening. The client is beginning to see that he is powerless over alcohol, and in admitting his powerlessness he will begin to seek something else to believe in. Can he trust that his God will restore his sanity *if* he admits his powerlessness? Almost everyone has feelings and thoughts about God or a higher power. One point you need to examine with your client is the difference between religion and spirituality. The client's last contact with God may have been as an angry teenager forced to attend church. Many people feel angry and let down by their God. We need to explore this difference with the client and inquire as to the image the client has of God.

Clients often feel relief in recognizing they have a disease because they are no longer to blame for their alcohol-related behavior. They are not bad, they merely have a bad disease. But, then, they blame God for giving them the disease in the first place. The client needs to explore the helpfulness of this belief for his recovery. Forgiveness, not anger, is going to give him freedom from his addiction. The client's higher power needs to become a source of positive strength and safety not a source of punishment and shame. Forgiveness takes time, a client cannot all of a sudden forgive God, himself, or other people in his life.

If you are not comfortable with the spiritual aspect, you may consider referring your client to clergy in his community as an adjunct to your counseling. Whereas we can provide internal and external structure through meetings and new belief systems, the safety provided by a belief in a God relates to the spiritual self of the person and gives the person a feeling of safety, security, and acceptance. The client believes on an emotional level that God will help him, if he asks for it.

Emotional/rational aspects, other than what we have already discussed, are not *the* focus. The client needs to hear that he is doing all he can do to get sober. The client needs to hear positive acceptance. The client will describe her feelings as "being on a roller coaster." We do not do a lot of feeling work at this point because the clients do not have the coping mechanisms needed to deal with feelings. If they are encouraged to get in touch with their anger or pain, having no way to handle the feelings, the clients will respond as they always have, by drowning the feelings with alcohol. They simply need to move forward within the structure that we have provided and with the feelings of trust, hope, and autonomy that we are positively reinforcing. We do not deny the client's feelings; we recognize the feeling but how we deal with it depends upon the urgency of the feeling and where the person is in recovery.

If the client is expressing feelings about us or feelings about people in his life *today,* then we help the client to develop more realistic expectations so that he does not run (escape in a self-destructive way) with his feelings. We can do this effectively by using RET. The client needs some quick and easy ways to deal with the feelings that come up in daily living, feelings that, in the past, led him straight to the nearest liquor store. For example, a client often gets angry because people in his life do not seem to appreciate how difficult it is for him to stay sober. Coworkers may order alcoholic drinks when they are out for dinner, or a spouse may leave some wine in the refrigerator or invite friends over and the friends may bring alcohol with them. We need to teach the client to identify and challenge his irrational expectations about other's behavior. We are asking in effect: "Why *should* the people in your life act the way you want them to act? It would be nice if they did but, of course, they will not always or even usually act the way you want them to. How can you not upset yourself about that reality?"

Expression of feelings within the context of the therapeutic relationship is encouraged because they can be handled safely within that relationship. This is one way the client is going to learn how to have intimate relationships. For example, clients often feel hurt and angry when they discover that we are not going to satisfy their dependency needs. We need to explore these feelings and expectations with the client.

In contrast to these feelings in the "here and now," feelings about past events, especially childhood events such as sexual abuse, cannot effectively be dealt with until the client has some means of handling these feelings. Moreover, we must always remember that our treatment objectives are dependent upon the stage of recovery. In Stage II, the goal is simply to stay sober and in counseling the addict, we do that which facilitates that goal. We acknowledge how painful such childhood events must be, but we point out that now is not the optimal time to begin working through that pain. We can say to our client: "The more sober time you have, the deeper the issues you will be able to handle."

Stage II Tasks

The primary tasks of Stage II involve the client's adherence to the treatment plan. Is the client following the spirit as well as the letter of the treatment plan? Is the client taking steps to separate from active friends or does he "just happen" to run into his old active buddies? Is he making a conscious effort to not start romantic/sexual involvements or is he already attending sober dances and spending his time at meetings checking out potential female partners? Does the client stay away from specified hangouts but then stop in at a new club or pool hall?

We need to constantly monitor the client's progress toward the treatment goals. We need to check in on the client's experience of his other treatment modalities. We can do this by exploring the client's beliefs and behaviors. The client is responding to his feelings about A.A. and alcoholics. Can he identify with their stories? If not, why not? Is he choosing meetings at which the alcoholics are so unlike himself that he does not have to identify with their stories? If he is addicted to other drugs, is he attending Narcotics Anonymous (N.A.)? Is it okay to be an alcoholic but not to be a drug addict? How does he feel about his sitting amongst the alcoholics? Does he sit at the back of the room or up front? Has he raised his hand to speak? Has he introduced himself to others? Does he have a sponsor? Has he asked for help? Is he attending consistently or is he beginning to slack off?

What are his feelings about group counseling, the group leader, and other members? Whom does he trust, whom does he mistrust, and on what does he base this judgment? What is his behavior in group therapy like? Is he an active member or a passive observer? Has he shared his feelings about being in treatment? Has he taken any risks? Has he cried? Has he confronted another member? Or, alternatively, is he just along for the ride with participation limited to throwing out a few A.A. slogans. These are questions we need to explore with our clients again and again because the answers tell us whether the client is simply complying or whether he is beginning to process what is going on.

We can help provide the external structure necessary to allow the client to begin to heal. As the client recognizes her loss of control and the unmanageability of her life, she is scared. We respond by suggesting ways she can structure her life in the form of attending A.A. meetings, developing an A.A. network, getting a sponsor, enjoying leisure-time activities, and obtaining individual and group counseling. We help develop internal structure by facilitating the development of healthy beliefs and challenging irrational beliefs. Slogans such as "Take it easy" and "One day at a time" are safe and reassuring to someone whose life has fallen apart.

Resistance and Solutions in Stage II

Resistance at Stage II generally results from the failure of the client to admit that he does have a problem with alcohol and must stop engaging in the compulsion if he is to get better. The denial system is still intact. The client agreed to try to quit, but chances are he was complying rather than believing that he needed to give up the addictive substance. The behavioral signs that denial is still intact become obvious over time, eventually erupting in the client's use of alcohol or another drug.

How do you know when the client is retreating to his denial system? One of the first signs is the client's failure to follow through with the treatment plan objectives. This is one reason you need a very concrete treatment plan. The client may have agreed to attend five meetings a week and now is only attending one or two. We need to address this "slippage" immediately.

We need to return again and again to the client's beliefs about his alcohol/drug use and the insidious belief that he can drink again. We need to go back and ask the same questions: "How do you know you are an alcoholic? What would you do if you did have a drink? What do you think would happen? Who would you tell if you had a drink? What would you do about it?" Because the addicted individual has lived in the extremes for so long, he applies this thinking to his own setbacks in recovery. If he has a drink he believes: "It is all over. I blew it, I might as well get really drunk now. There is no sense in going back to counseling now that I have blown it." Uncovering and teaching the client how to challenge this nonsense is essential to recovery.

The client needs to believe that no matter what he does, he needs to get back on track. If he drinks, he must tell someone immediately: his counselor, his sponsor, his group. Keeping such a secret is deadly to recovery. If the client says that he would not tell anyone because of his shame, then you can show the client that he has not accepted his loss of control over the drug, he has not accepted his alcoholism. They say that alcoholism is a disease of relapse and you need to show your client that he is not bad because he is an alcoholic. The question is: "What are you going to do about it now that it has happened?" The only thing the client can do now is put down the alcohol/drug and try again.

Use of Contracts.   One way to deal with the fear of, or actuality of, slips and relapses is with a contract or written agreement. You may consider a written emergency plan or contract stating specifically what the client will do if he drinks or takes drugs. This is especially important for clients who have attempted suicide or who say they will kill themselves if they drink again. Some clients will tell you, "I don't have another recovery in me." They believe, magically, that this belief is keeping them sober. It is not keeping them sober and, not only that, relapses are always a possibility and they need to prepare for that possibility before it happens. You must discuss slips and relapse with all your clients, regardless of whether they are following through with the treatment plan. When a slip does occur, the client has a plan to follow that will lead him back to counseling and sobriety.

Slips and relapses need to be treated as learning experiences. The client needs to be asked what he has learned from the slip. You will ask the client what he thinks needs to change in the treatment plan and within himself. If the client continues to fail to follow through then you know that denial is still intact.

One question I am always asked is: How many times does the client need to slip or relapse before you decide that treatment is not working for this client at this time? That is, of course, a very individual decision and has to do with the specifics of the case. Is the client under a "Return-to-Work" agreement that states how slips and relapses are to be handled? Is the client in a high-risk occupation in which there is a great likelihood that someone is going to get hurt if your client uses drugs or alcohol on the job? Obviously, if your client is an airline pilot, bus driver, or medical professional, then the risk is greater than it is if he is in another occupation. You have less leeway in deciding how to handle slips and relapses when you are dealing with clients in high-risk occupations.

We need to consider whether the problem is in the treatment plan or whether the problem is in the client's behavior. Since we are only talking about the first three to six months (getting the structure in place and seeing if it works), it should become pretty obvious in a short period of time whether or not the client is going to respond to this treatment method.

If the client slips more than once in the first three months, the prognosis for sobriety does not look good. How you respond to the slip depends on whether or not the client was following the treatment plan and had a slip anyway or whether the client was not following the treatment plan. If the client was stopping in at the local pub to order a Coke and a sandwich, then the problem is pretty obvious. He is not following the spirit of the treatment plan, denial is intact. We need to discuss with the client the question of why he is setting himself up to drink? If the client was following the treatment plan and still had a slip, then that is a different problem requiring further changes in the treatment plan.

10

Stage III: Working and Playing Sober

Stage III involves the client's fitting work and play into sobriety. This stage begins anywhere from one to three months and continues to one year. The time depends, in part, on the type of occupation the client has and whether or not the client is able to return to that job at this time. Learning to play sober needs to begin within the first three months. The process of this stage is the psychosocial crisis of initiative versus guilt. The potential strengths are purpose and competence versus inhibition and inertia. The client is saying, "I have stopped drinking, now what? I know how to be an alcoholic in recovery, now how do I deal with the real world." The client needs to begin to rid himself of some guilt because guilt and feelings of being "less than" tie up the recovering person's energy and keep him from moving forward. The client is learning to get to know who he is without alcohol/drugs.

Three Aspects of Self

The cognitive aspect continues to be primary. In helping the client rid himself of the guilt, we can focus on the concept of alcoholism. The client did not choose to be an alcoholic and were he not an alcoholic, he would not have done a lot of the hurtful things he did to others and to himself. The client begins to admit he is alcoholic. Will the client move forward and do what he needs to do to live a sober way of life? Or, alternatively, will he stagnate and regress to the denial that tells him: "It wasn't that bad." "You are not like 'them' (i.e., alcoholics)." "You can learn to control your drinking."

The spiritual aspect is coming to the fore as the client reexperiences his fear of others and feelings of shame in returning to social circles and the workplace. You will find that your clients are asking their higher power for help more and more frequently and most are discovering that they get the help they need when they do ask. They need this feeling of trust in taking on the new challenges of social activities and work. Through this experience they often do come to believe in a higher power restoring them to sanity. At this point in recovery, clients will begin returning to church and contacting clergy from their past.

The emotional/relational aspect does not change much during this phase. As a counselor you continue to use the cognitive techniques, help the client follow through with the treatment plan, and offer the client your encouragement. We always focus on the client's strengths and potential and we do a lot of what is called *strength confrontation,* which involves confronting the client with strengths that he denies he has.

Stage III Tasks

Stage III is very task-oriented because this stage involves the client doing a lot of legwork as he expands his recovery sphere to include work and social life. Psychoeducation continues with the client becoming educated on the disease concept and beginning to believe, not just intellectually, but emotionally, that he does have the disease of addiction. The process of moving the belief from an intellectual to an emotional level involves working on the first three steps. In addition to this psychological and spiritual work, the client is returning to his workplace as a sober person. He is also returning to his family as a sober parent and to his social life as a sober friend. Learning to work and play sober are major hurdles for the newly recovering person.

Learning to Play in Sobriety

Humor as Therapy. Teaching the client how to play as a sober person is one of the more enjoyable aspects of recovery counseling. There are two types of play in recovery. There is play that involves activities that the client needs to do for fun and relaxation and there is the play involved in developing a sense of humor about oneself, others, and life in general. I do not think that there is a more essential component in counseling than humor. Part of facilitating the capacity to play involves developing a sense of humor. Helping the client to lighten up and laugh at his and others' human capacity for making mistakes enables the client to let go of some of his perfectionism and self-criticism. Spontaneity returns and the client can begin to take risks with himself in the play arena that he is not ready to take in the work arena.

Ellis (1977a, 1977b), has pioneered the use of humor as a method of psychotherapy. Ellis et al. (1988) write, "Humor is often a fine antidote against disturbance and compulsion because it has a powerful emotive as well as cognitive element. Laughter can dramatically jolt your clients out of their self-defeating habits and cleverly push them into anti-addictive action." Perhaps what I find most amazing in my work as a therapist is how a simple phrase or comment given at just the right moment, an unexpected moment, can break through denial in a way that months of empathic listening cannot. The phrase is most useful when it does not fit neatly into the client's belief system.

Humor can challenge our defense system in a way that simple confrontation cannot. Because it is humor, it is not as threatening. Humor allows the person to see things in a totally new light. Think about your own experiences with humor and how it has helped you accept reality. The people I learn the most from and enjoy the most are the ones who push me to see things in a totally different light; they do this with humor. But remember, as with comedy in general, timing is everything. You need to learn when and what type of humor to use. There is a fine line between "making fun of" the client's beliefs in a way that is shaming versus bringing the client along with you to find the humor in his beliefs. Sarcasm is not an appropriate form of humor in the therapeutic setting.

A sense of humor is as important for you, as a counselor, as it is for the client. The counselor needs a sense of humor as a survival method in recovery counseling and he needs a sense of humor in order to help facilitate the client's use of humor. I do not know whether you can develop a sense of humor on your own. Fortunately, at least in my experience, those counselors and therapists who are able to survive and thrive in the field of addictions seem to have a well-developed sense of humor. They may have entered the field with it and it may have also become more developed along the way as an adaptive mechanism. If you do not have a sense of humor, listening to some of Ellis's (1977b) rational humorous songs, which he uses as a part of psychotherapy with his clients, may be of help to you in developing one.

Much of human behavior when viewed from the outside is humorous. We can all recall arguing with a loved one over something ridiculous. At the time we are angry, but a month later we cannot even recall what the argument was about. This behavior, when viewed in retrospect, looks childish to us, and it is. The person has no perspective at the time; all he can focus on are *his* feelings, *his* wants.

The positive side to childish behavior is that it shows the person can get in touch with what John Bradshaw refers to as the "inner child." Perhaps only an angry, hurt inner child, initially, but in time other aspects will also emerge: the more spontaneous, fun-loving, joyful child. Getting in touch with the inner child serves several functions. The client learns to differentiate between childish and childlike behavior and now knowing the difference can allow himself to be childlike when appropriate. This introduction to the playful child will help in later stages as the client works on healing the pain of the inner child. By recognizing childish behavior as that of his "inner child" and not that of his "adult" self, the client can begin to learn how to satisfy the needs of the inner child while responding to the situation with his adult self.

Play as a Treatment Goal

The cognitive aspect has to do with the recovering person's lack of self-acceptance. Because they do not view themselves as worthy, they are not motivated to do anything for themselves that involves just having fun. The unhealthy belief is that: "I am not worth it. I have already wasted enough time on myself indulging in my addiction, now it's time for me to work." We need to challenge these beliefs by showing the client that he is worth it, and that in order for his recovery to continue he needs to learn how to relax and enjoy himself. Also, if the client does not learn how to relax and have fun, he may channel that energy into work or another compulsion and then you simply have a new addiction.

Clients typically do not have a well-developed concept of fun or leisure that is not connected to drinking/drugging. In treatment planning, you develop play objectives just as you do any other objective. The activity must not involve alcohol, it is best if done with at least one other person, and it needs to be potentially enjoyable for the client. Play can be as simple as going to the movies, going shopping or to a museum, or going out for lunch with a friend.

Play can combine different aspects of the self: social, emotional, and physical; for example, joining a health club. Often you need to also encourage the clients to *use* the health club after they have joined because they will otherwise not take the time. Lost hobbies or sports are also excellent, such as playing golf, tennis, boating, and roller skating. Drawing out the client's imagination and creativity can be done through photography, art, or dance classes. In time, you need to work on the client to take a vacation and then you need to plan for him to have fun on his vacation.

Learning to Work Sober

The work area is also very important for client's self-esteem and self-confidence. The individual needs to develop or reidentify a sense of competence and purpose. As discussed earlier, we need to be aware of many factors in helping the client deal with the career issue. We need to know how the workplace perceives his addiction, or if it even knows about it. We need to know how the client feels about his job, the stresses on the job, and whether or not he feels safe returning to the same job site and occupation. When, where, and how the person returns to work today also has to do with what type of treatment he received and what the insurance company is willing to provide as far as aftercare (e.g., outpatient group and individual counseling).

The work-specific cognitive aspect has to do with challenging feelings of shame and anger, low self-worth, fear of failure, and fear of drinking/drugging on-the-job. Feelings of shame and guilt connect back to a failure to accept that one is an alcoholic, and an alcoholic is not a bad person but a person with a disease.

Fear of using also has to do with acceptance that one has a disease and one needs to plan accordingly to deal with feelings and urges while on the job. Fear of failure on the job has to do with this irrational notion that many people suffer from: "I must do my job perfectly and if I do not, I am a bad, worthless human being."

Another very common issue that crops up along with feelings of worthlessness on the job is assertiveness. Often clients view themselves as second-class citizens and thus do not have a good balance between putting others' needs above their own and aggressively taking what they need. I recommend that you work on assertiveness with the client so you can teach him how to get along with others and still get his professional needs met.

Resistance and Solutions

Resistance in Stage III comes in the form of a fearful *"I can't"* rather than the defiant *"I won't"* of previous stages. The client is afraid of failing in his tasks of returning to work or of play. Because of the level of awareness he has already gained and his relationship with you, the client is less able to use defiance but more able to rely on his old behavior of helpless, hopeless dependence in hopes that you will rescue him. I have discussed possible solutions to this form of resistance under cognitive techniques, but, most simply put, I always come back to the same question: "What are you willing to do to stay sober?" Because it is not that you *cannot*, it is that you *will not*. Maybe you *cannot* envision yourself sober for the rest of your life but: "You *can* ask a friend out for coffee," "You *can* speak to your boss about getting out of work early on Wednesdays," and so on.

Return-to-Work Issues. Most often the employer does not even know that the employee has received treatment for an addiction. In that case, you and the client work out the recovery plan together. When the workplace does know that the employee is in recovery, this creates a whole new set of issues. In addition to excuses that recovery is interfering with work are the excuses that work is interfering with recovery. Some clients will use recovery as an excuse for not doing their share of the work. Unfortunately, some bosses and employee assistance programs will enable this type of behavior by allowing it to continue. The boss wants to be a "nice guy" and he thinks he is doing all he can to help his employee get back on his feet. The boss does not realize that he is doing a disservice to himself, his company, his other employees, and to the recovering person.

The recovering person needs to be held accountable for his share of the work. In addition to that, he needs to feel as though people do have confidence in his abilities and do expect him to perform up to his capabilities. Many brilliant and gifted people have talents that are never realized because they have been so "protected" at their workplace. The workplace employees and colleagues are so afraid of losing the person to alcohol/drugs again that they remove all the challenge from that person's career. One of the greatest harms we can do to a person is to expect little from him.

The other side of the expectation coin is expecting too much. Another danger in the recovering person's return to work is a "setup" by the workplace. Coworkers may set the person up to fail because they are angry at her or because they want to get her out of their organization. The setting up of a person usually involves overloading her with work or treating her in a negative way because she is an alcoholic. Both can drive the person back to the drug and out of work. For instance, a nurse may be set up by returning her to a hospital floor on which she has access to medication or to a floor where everyone knows she was caught diverting (stealing) drugs from work and then treat her badly because of that.

We need to find a balance between these two extremes of underworking and overworking the newly recovering employee. The returning person needs to return slowly. She needs to be updated on the events and information she missed while she was away. She needs to be told specifically what her job description is. Medical people need to have either no access or only limited access to psychoactive medication when returning to work and this needs to be worked out with the direct supervisor. Over time, job restrictions need to be lifted as the returning person gains back her responsibilities of the job. She needs to be shown that she is gaining back the trust of her boss and coworkers. Over time, the person needs to be considered for and offered promotions based on job performance, just like any other employee.

In addition to work performance expectations are the expectations that the counselor, the workplace, and the client have with regard to recovery. Recovery can take many forms. Employees do not need to get out of work early every night to attend A.A. or group counseling. However, some consideration needs to be given to the employee and her treatment. A request to get out of work early one night a week for treatment purposes is not unreasonable, as long as the employee offers to make up the time. Compromises must be reached to prevent resentment from growing and it is best if they are reached prior to the person's return to the workplace. Not only can the employer come to resent the recovering person but coworkers will resent the "special" treatment she gets and will make the job environment a living hell. Soon the workplace is operating like one big dysfunctional family. The recovering person will be the scapegoat in this family, a role that is all too familiar and one which will lead back to active addiction.

Use of Contracts. An effective way to deal with return-to-work issues involves drawing up a contract or agreement between the workplace (boss, direct supervisor), the client, and the counselor. An example of a return-to-work agreement is included in Appendix C. In preparing this contract, each person writes out her specific role and expectations. Compromises are then reached. Each person understands the procedure to be followed when conditions of the contract are broken. Your client knows up front what will happen if she takes a drink or drug. The workplace knows how to deal with work performance problems and whom to contact when there is a problem with which they cannot deal. Everyone involved feels more comfortable knowing where they stand.

11

Stages IV and V: Identity and Intimacy in Recovery

Note that the identity and intimacy development of Stages IV and V is specific to recovery, that is, for the purposes of recovery rather than that which occurs as a function of normal development across the life span. For instance, the identity I am talking about in this stage has to do with the recovering person's identity as an alcoholic, not a more general identity question of "Who am I?"

Stage IV: Identity Development Specific to Recovery

The psychosocial crisis of Stage IV is identity vs. identity confusion. The potential strength is fidelity versus repudiation. The resolution of this crisis typically occurs between years one and two. The crucial aspect of Stage IV involves the client's *acceptance* that she is an alcoholic. The client is saying, "I am an alcoholic but I have the tools to know how to deal with my alcoholism and that is okay." This is not to say that the client feels good about being an alcoholic; typically this comes much later in recovery. In fact, there is often a letdown around the first year sober date because the client thinks that "This is the way it is. This is the way my life needs to be in order for me to stay sober." That is pretty overwhelming for the client who has just struggled through the first year.

Nor am I suggesting that the recovering person does not backslide after she has reached this point. Recovery is a process; clients continue to move forward and backward as they are affected by internal and external stressors. Hopefully, they will have learned to cope with stressors without resorting to their addiction. Possibly the biggest mistake we make as therapists is to assume that there is a "cure" for this disease. We begin to move on to other areas and we neglect the client's sobriety. We need to continue to check in on our client's sobriety even after three years or fifteen years.

On the positive side, the strength emerging in Stage IV is fidelity. The recovering person has faith that recovery holds promises, faith in a higher power, and faith in the self-help program. A marker of this transition is the client's ability to utilize not only our guidance but also to branch out and use mentors and leaders. The negative potential outcome of this stage is role repudiation: a diffidence or defiance in relation to available identity potential, according to Erikson (1982). The client who does not utilize mentors in the program as part of his *recovery identity* often shows a great deal of anger and begins to put down the membership or attack aspects of the program.

Three Aspects of Self

The spiritual self is primary during Stage IV as the recovering person chooses between turning over her will to a higher power and taking that will back. She struggles with her faith in God, A.A., and herself, as she asks: "Will I accept this identity as an alcoholic or will I return to my denial and believe that I can continue to drink/drug?" This question is, of course, not entirely a conscious one. A marker for this transition is the client's asking for help and letting God decide what the form of help will be versus asking for specific things: people (love objects) and things (job, material gain). Those who are asking for things and expressing anger when they do not get what they want, have not turned over their will.

The cognitive aspect does not change in this stage. You continue to work with the alcoholic in challenging her unhealthy beliefs about self and others. The emotional/relational aspect also continues as in the previous stage. Every client is an individual and responds differently to the first year of sobriety, but there are some general markers. From my experience, clients either respond with joy or sadness to this stage. Those who respond with joy are generally clients who did not make it to a year in their previous sobriety attempts. Those with sadness or apathy tend to be younger, and to them the thought of facing a lifetime of sobriety as it was in the first year is, indeed, sad. The quality of sobriety is obviously higher for those who are enjoying their sobriety, but that does not mean that those clients who are feeling down are in trouble with regard to their recovery. Based on my experience, this feeling response is less a predictor of future sobriety as an indication of past attempts.

On a cognitive level, you can respond to the overwhelmingness of a lifetime of recovery by pointing out that every year recovery gets better with more rewards. You can also remind the client of the meaning of the A.A. slogan: "One day at a time." Counseling groups and support groups are crucial at this time as this is where the recovering person hears that others share these feelings, and they can reassure the recovering person that as long as they do not drink/drug things will get better.

Stage IV Tasks

In Stage IV, the client continues to work with the counselor on challenging unhealthy beliefs about self. The client is learning not only to admit that she is an alcoholic but to accept this fact and learn how to integrate that component of self into her larger identity. With that acceptance, the client begins to focus on taking care of herself. She works on developing self-esteem and expressing her knowledge about self (feelings, wants, and needs). She continues to work on Step Two and Three as she begins to identify and connect with her spiritual self. Much of the task-work in Stage IV actually involves tasks to be completed by the counselor as she deals with various forms of client resistance.

Resistance and Solutions

The client's potential defiance presents itself in various forms. As with all previous stages, we need to pay attention primarily to the client's behavior and not her words. Behavioral markers include the following: Is the client sticking to the treatment plan? Is the client still afraid of alcohol, as he should be, or has he begun testing his disease by stopping off at the local pub for a

Coke or going out with friends to a club after work? Has the client begun to internalize the identity of the A.A. group? Does the client express the "need" for a meeting without your suggesting it? Does the client belong to a group? Do the people in his group have his phone number and do they ask him where he has been when he fails to show up for a meeting? Does he celebrate his one-year sobriety anniversary with his group or does he fail to do anything on his anniversary?

Erikson speaks of the importance of mentorship in identity development, and we can apply this to recovery as well. The use of mentors is particularly telling because much of the addict's battle has to do with the control and defiance against authorities. If this struggle has not been resolved, the client will be unable or unwilling to use mentors. You need to know the answers to the following questions: Does the client have a sponsor and how does she feel about her sponsor? Does she call her sponsor only when she has things under control? What does your client do when she becomes really stressed out and feels like picking up a drink/drug? Does she call you or her sponsor or does she isolate and then tell you about it a week later when she has "fixed it"? How does she feel about other people in the program giving her suggestions or confronting her? Does she utilize feedback by putting it into action or does she just give it lip service?

As counselors, we are also authority figures and, as such, our clients sometimes react defiantly to our suggestions. If your client does not express anger overtly, she may do it passively. Passive aggression or anger may come in the form of her not following the treatment plan, in her not paying you on time, or in canceling appointments at the last minute. I find defiance often comes out in the form of sarcastic humor. There is nothing wrong with our clients' feeling anger towards us. In fact, if they never feel anger towards us, my feeling is that we are not hitting the right buttons. Our clients are going to hear feedback that they do not want to look at, and sometimes they are going to get angry at us for pointing this vulnerability out to them. The problem is not the client's anger, it is how the client manages her anger. We need to teach the client how to identify her angry feelings, their source, and how to express them appropriately (i.e., so that they will be heard).

Is the client doing her homework or is she making excuses?

Does she agree to do her homework and then come back week after week not "having had the time" to follow through? How do you deal with this resistance? You rely on your relationship with the client, which is why it is so important that you *have* established a relationship with the client. Rather than focus on the content (no time to do homework) and spending the session problem solving with the client (scheduling her day for her), you focus on the process of what is going on in the therapeutic relationship. How do these resistant behaviors affect the therapeutic relationship? If the client agrees to homework and then does not do it, you may ask the client what this says about her trust in you as a counselor and the strength of her commitment to sobriety.

Slips and Relapses.   Slips and relapses need to be used as learning experiences. If the client has stayed sober for a year, we can say that he "has the tools" to not use. So why did he use? We need to focus more and more on what his returning to his addictive behavior has to say about his motivation to sobriety and about his level of trust in those who are helping him with his sobriety. For instance, consider the following scenario: a client discusses with you a getaway weekend in which there is the possibility of drug use. The two of you agree that going on the trip would be too risky. In his next session, he reports that he did go on the trip and he did use drugs.

What does such resistance say about your counseling relationship and the client's level of commitment to sobriety? By focusing on the relationship, we avoid blaming the client. The client is responsible for his bad choices, but he is not a bad person. If you focus on "the badness" of your client, your client is going to feel "bad," not badly but *bad* as in shameful. You cannot beat your client into sobriety, he must go willingly. If your client feels "bad," he will get as angry at you as he did at his parents and he will then have a reason (albeit irrational) not to trust you.

Splitting.   Another sign of resistance which appears anytime in the first year is what we call "splitting." Splitting involves the client's setting up her mentors in opposition to one another so that she does not have to take responsibility for her unhealthy behavior. The client is essentially playing one counselor against another. This is especially common in addictions (be it with food or chemicals) in which clients tend to be involved with more than one helping system. For example, the client may have you as a primary counselor, a different counselor as group leader, a counselor for each of her children involved in the Department of Social Services system, and a medical professional who may advocate the use of medication as a "cure" for the addiction.

The client splits these authorities by distorting or misrepresenting to one professional what another professional is saying about the client's treatment. This allows the client to feel "special" and powerful while not taking responsibility for her treatment. This behavior harks back to playing one parent against another in order to feel "special," and is also a continuation of a lifelong technique of avoiding responsibility by blaming flawed (nonperfect) authorities.

Splitting is extremely common, as well as aggravating, in inpatient treatment programs in which the client works with several counselors as well and also goes to outside meetings. The client will disagree with what you are saying by quoting another staff member who has expressed a belief contrary to yours. Or the client will attempt to be a "special" or "privileged" client by showing other clients and staff how his relationship with you is somehow more special than their relationship with you.

Splitting is best dealt with by the professionals together confronting the client. Of course, if the staff members *are* playing favorites or if they side with the splitting client without checking out the client's claims with the staff first, then they are as unhealthy as the client and the client's unhealthy behavior cannot be worked through. The client learns nothing about her behavior and may even be discharged from an inpatient facility for this form of resistance if the staff becomes too overwhelmed. Before taking as truth what your client says about another professional, "consider the source" as we say, the source being the patient or client. Check it out yourself with the other professionals involved.

A form of splitting may also occur between you and A.A. members or sponsors, especially if you are not in recovery yourself. The client may passively attack you by quoting something she heard in A.A. For instance, she may have heard that counseling or psychotherapy is not a good thing, or she may say that "civilians" just can't understand the disease. Or the client may begin to distance himself from the program by "hearing what he wants to hear" which generally involves taking things out of context. He sets you up against the program and then tries to gain your alliance against the program.

To help you deal with this manipulation, picture the client as an angry little kid who does not want to do chores. He is standing in the middle of two parents who cannot agree on child rearing and who are also angry at each other. Addicted clients, generally, are also co-dependent and they are very good at tuning into our vulnerabilities and fears and using these as a way to avoid taking responsibility. The client gets the two parents fighting and then slips out the back to do what he wants to do. If the parents later confront him on his failure to do his chores, whom can they hold accountable? Let's not get caught up in debating whose approach to sobriety is the better one. Given the number of active addicts, it's clear that no one has found "the cure." I also remind my clients that even Bill W. (a founder of A.A.) was in psychotherapy.

Stage V: Intimacy Development Specific to Recovery

The intimacy in Stage V has to do with developing and maintaining friendships not the intimacy of romantic/sexual relationships. The psychosocial crisis for this stage is intimacy versus isolation. The potential strengths are love versus exclusivity. The resolution of this stage typically occurs from year one to years two and three. The recovering person needs to learn how to get his or her social needs met. Relationships are very difficult for recovering persons, in general. They struggle with issues of control and assertiveness. They often ask whether they should voice their feelings about something or whether they should hold back and let it pass. This stage is very important because it is at this stage that the client generally begins to get in touch with "old" feelings of abandonment, betrayal, and shame. How your client deals with these feelings can make or break his recovery.

Three Aspects of Self

The primary aspect of this stage is spiritual and relational/emotional. What is really put to the test is the client's faith. Although the client may say that he has faith in a higher power, when it comes to relationships this faith is tested. Many clients will sell their faith short in order to have the relationship they *want* regardless of whether it is good for their recovery. This is particularly true if they feel they are in love with this other person. The client has the opportunity to work on honesty and trust. Now the client has let go of the need to control drugs and alcohol, she needs to let go of the need to control others. This is a very difficult challenge.

Stage V Tasks

There is a broad range of tasks that may be included in the intimacy stage of recovery. The client is working on maintaining his recovery program and, at this same time, moving on to incorporate more of life's experiences into his program of recovery. Tasks for this stage include relapse prevention work. In relapse prevention work, we help the client identify situations that threaten his sobriety. The assumption behind relapse prevention is that there are clear warning signs that the client is going to drink or use drugs months prior to his actually doing so. Warning signs or "triggers" may come in form of behavior (getting away from meetings), attitude (resentful, self-pitying), or feelings (anger, depression, sadness, fear). Often clues to the client's triggers can be gained from his past slips and relapses. We help the client write out the beliefs and feelings involved in high-risk situations. We teach the client how to avoid these situations or, if he finds himself in a high-risk situation, how to cope without resorting to taking a drink or a drug. The client learns to identify the warning signs of his "budding" (building up to drink) and what to do about it when he is aware of these signs. There are many resources available on relapse prevention (e.g., Maultsby, 1978).

In addition to identifying and watching for the warning signs of relapse, the client is taking steps to further his involvement in recovery. He does this by *joining* a self-help group and a Step Group, and going on speaking engagements or "commitments" with his group. He may begin to go on A.A. retreats or conventions. He is working on getting honest with himself and others through his counseling and support groups. He is socializing with friends, family, and relatives and he is beginning to identify his co-dependent behaviors as he does so.

Resistance and Solutions

Much of the work during this stage has to do with exploring how clients feel about the way they are treated by others. Clients seem very angry, and in time they come to see that beneath this anger often lay hurt. This stage involves asking the clients questions about how they felt when their friend, spouse, or child, said what they did or treated them the way that they did and why they felt this way. Relationships are a way for the client to get in touch with beliefs and feelings he has previously denied. For example, your client may deny that he seeks others' approval but that is tested in relationships. He sees in relationships that he really does deny his true feelings in order to be liked by other people. You continue to work on identifying and challenging irrational beliefs and feelings.

Issues of co-dependency become more obvious at this stage of recovery. Clients take responsibility for others' feelings and place them above their own. They may begin to agree to sponsor too many people or they may begin counseling other people in a half-way house in their free time. They may begin going to their spouse's meetings or criticizing their spouse's recovery. They are angry at their sponsor (and often their counselor) for not being able to help them. In short, they may begin spending all their time, energy, and finances helping others' sobriety while neglecting their own. They begin to feel guilt-ridden and angry and overwhelmed as the boundaries between themselves and others crumble.

We need to help clients set limits on their caretaking. For instance, clients may cut back on or stop sponsoring people. We may also begin to explore their role in their family of origin. Possibly they were the caretaker in the family and the only way they know how to connect with others is by taking care of them. They only feel good about themselves when they are needed by others. We are only just beginning to look to their childhood. We are beginning to ask how this present behavior relates to their role in their family of origin. We are setting the stage for the clients to connect their childhood experiences with their present unresolved conflicts.

Up to this point, we have dealt with inappropriate feelings by challenging the belief system. That is, you may challenge the belief that the boss *should* always be fair. Now you are saying, "I wonder where those beliefs came from. I wonder how fair your parents were in the treatment of you and your siblings?" Now that the client has some way of coping with his feelings, you encourage the client to get in touch with his feelings and "sit with them," i.e., feel and process through these feelings. The client is preparing to move on to the next stage, which involves getting back in touch with the self she lost so long ago and learning about her needs as separate from the needs of others.

12

Stages VI and VII: Identity and Intimacy Development

Stage VI: Identity Development

In Stage VI, the internal and external structures you and your client have set up are working and the client is maintaining sobriety. The client has achieved some measure of safety in sobriety. As long as the client does not neglect his recovery plan, he can now begin to explore additional aspects of self. This stage relates, then, to a more general knowledge about self rather than a self only in relation to sobriety. The crisis is the same: identity versus identity confusion with the emerging strength of fidelity versus repudiation. The resolution of this stage generally takes place between years three and five. The counseling or therapy in Stage VI is not much different from counseling an individual who is not in recovery. Counselors who are trained to deal only with addiction may want to consider referring the client to a more generally trained counselor at this point, depending on the issue at hand and level of competence in handling that issue.

Several issues do occur more often in the recovering client. Most likely, the person came from a dysfunctional home with one or two alcoholic parents. There are issues such as abuse and neglect. You need to explore the role your client played in this dysfunctional system. Working through the impact of the dysfunctional parent(s) on your client is important because very often these clients have not separated from this system. In educating yourself and your client on the roles adult children play in their family of origin, I recommend Claudia Black (1981) and John Bradshaw (1988).

The client needs to separate psychologically from the family system of origin, if it continues to be an unhealthy one, in order to get free of his compulsion. Because the system is sick, it is your client and not the sick family system who must set limits. Often the client is drawn back into the system out of guilt and shame. For example, if your client always played the scapegoat, she continues to be every member's excuse for the problems in their lives. They do not want your client to escape this role because then they would have to look at themselves. You must help your client to see that she needs to give up this identity as a scapegoat, and part of doing so is letting go of the sick family system that continues to reinforce this negative identity.

Separating from unhealthy loved ones brings up feelings of loss, and these feelings connect back to childhood losses. You begin to discuss losses that result from being brought up in a dysfunctional home. The client missed out on having a healthy parent-child relationship. Often the client was active through junior high and high school and missed out on that part of his life as well. Kübler-Ross's (1969) book *On Death and Dying* is helpful in identifying where the client is in the process of grieving these losses.

Until the client is free of his sick family, it is very difficult for him to not bring this sickness into his next intimate relationship or his own family system. At first this process is only intellectual. Later on, the client becomes aware of the continuing impact of his family of origin on his present relationships. He then begins to have feelings about his family of origin.

Issues of co-dependence continue to be dealt with in this stage. The client begins to explore how she defines herself in relation to others, e.g., as a mother, a wife, a career-person, a daughter. We need to find the answers to the following questions: Where does this client get her self-esteem? What are her strengths? Does she have a view of herself separate from those she takes care of, or is defined by? Or, alternatively, does she continue to live a role-defined existence with no awareness of boundaries between self and others? Co-dependence, in my opinion, is more a problem of identity and individuation than a problem of intimacy. The person continues to define herself through others and get her needs met through the taking care of others. In working on this, you focus not on the relationship but on what the client is avoiding within herself.

Three Aspects of Self

The emotional/relational aspect becomes primary, as does the spiritual. At this point, the approach shifts somewhat from a cognitive approach to a more emotional approach. Bradshaw's books and exercises are very helpful in working through feelings about ourselves and the roles we played in our family of origin and continue to play in our relationships today. Many clients are not in touch with their inner child. Getting the client to pay attention to the child within helps the client focus on her needs and not on the needs of the family of origin or her new intimate relationships.

The spiritual aspect shows itself in the client's willingness to move beyond a focus on how not to use the addictive substance to how to grow and realize his potential. As they say, this requires a "leap of faith" similar to the leap of faith required in giving up the dependence on a substance. Now the person is asked to give up much of what he knows to be his identity. This identity may be negative but it is all he has. The client is now saying, "I am more than just an alcoholic, I am also a human being with all sorts of strengths and weaknesses and I need to begin identifying those."

Another issue is giving up other obsessive-compulsive behaviors such as smoking or overeating. Clients will generally bring up the desire to give up these other compulsions themselves. They need to approach these compulsions in the same way they approached chemical dependence, the obvious difference being that they do not necessarily abstain from these other compulsions. For instance, in a food addiction the client needs to begin to pay attention to her internal cues (thoughts, feelings) when she begins to overeat.

Another issue specific to chemical dependence is a delayed adolescence. If your client has a long history of drinking/drugging, then he or she is probably developmentally delayed. For example, a thirty-year-old may only be at the adolescent stage of psychosocial development because of the interrupting effects of alcohol/drugs. So it is appropriate that she is having an identity crisis and is trying to find herself in her relationships with others, especially adolescent love/sexual relationships. The goal at this point is to help her keep from losing herself, her identity as a separate individual, in these relationships, and to support her in her search for a new identity.

Often clients in the third and fourth years begin to get down on themselves for not being age-appropriate. They say things like, "I'm thirty years old, I should be married with kids now, not asking who I am!" You need to point out the developmental periods that they missed and the need for them to take their time in finding out who they are and what they want and need.

Clients often begin to question their careers at this stage. Many clients will return to school to further themselves in their present field or to change fields or to find out what school is like when you are not high on alcohol and drugs. This can be a very healthy experience that boosts self-image and self-esteem as the client realizes that she has not lost her capacity to think, and that she can make it in school without the aid of drugs. For others, returning to school is necessary because they have lost their means of support. They may have lost their financial support because they supported themselves through the selling of drugs, they have left a dangerous living situation where they were supported by a partner, or because they cannot return to their old career (their license has been revoked or the risk is too great).

Stage VI Tasks

Identity development tasks include all those things that the client needs to do in order to find out more about himself. In order to further focus on himself, he works on giving up his remaining addictions: food, smoking, workaholism, co-dependent behavior. He identifies and deals with family of origin issues: adult child of an alcoholic issues, sexual abuse, and so on. He learns to identify the role he played in the family and how he has continued to play out this role in his life today. He learns to stop doing that. It is no longer okay for him to be the scapegoat in his family of origin or in his workplace. He is able to identify and accept his strengths and weaknesses. He begins to question his satisfaction with his career and education and looks to adjust these areas to find a better fit with his new knowledge about self. He may return to school to finish a degree or begin to look for a job that better suits his needs.

Resistance and Solutions

Clients often resist moving forward to this stage out of fear of failure. They have found some safety in defining themselves as "recovering alcoholics," and now we are asking them to expand on their identities. Resistance comes in several forms. They may return to their addictive behavior, they may develop other compulsions or defiant behavior, or they may become stuck at a self-focused or role-focused level of development. Clients will resist this stage by regressing to other forms of dependency. Sometimes they will even verbalize their resistance by saying things like, "I'm not as healthy as you think I am!" From my experience, many people do not positively resolve this stage. They may stay rigidly stuck; they do not necessarily return to their addictive behavior.

Within these psychosocial stages of identity and intimacy are developmental levels. These levels include self-focused, role-focused, and individuated-connected. Notice that in the intimacy measure presented in the next stage, there is a "conventional" or "role-defined" level of intimacy in which the majority of people, as a society not just those in recovery, get stuck. There is also a role-defined level of identity. Simply put, people stop asking questions about their existence and they simply work with what they have. They lack awareness into their internal selves. People in recovery have achieved a "role-defined" identity in the form of "I am a recovering alcoholic" and they do not necessarily move beyond that stage.

When a client does not positively resolve this stage by integrating other identity components into his image of self, often what you see is a juvenile cliquishness. This cliquishness is evident when A.A. is used as a social club and, as with all social clubs, it functions partly so that the few who belong can exclude the many who do not. The behavior of these cliques is not much different than that which we all experienced in high school. The focus is on the external self: compulsively buying the right clothes, exercising at the right fitness clubs, going to the right vacation resorts. Improved outward appearance is a positive indicator of recovery, but it needs to reflect an improved self-image not substitute for it.

One danger of staying at a role-focused level is that often negative identity elements are also present. This negative identity represents the anger or defiance that the client has not worked through. Let me give you an example. One client of mine knew the lingo of the program inside and out. She was educated and successful and she had recently married a recovering addict who was now also successful. But she could not give up the control necessary to move on developmentally. She was hooked on an active life-style even though she was no longer actively using chemicals. She held onto her control (and fears and anger) by resuming her cigarette smoking and by being co-dependently involved with nonrecovering addicts. She continues to live two lives: the perfect girl in recovery and the bad girl acting out her defiance. She does not yet have the "leap of faith" needed to give up her compulsions and look at the void that is within herself.

There is a certain "blindness" or lack of awareness in people at the role-focused and self-focused levels. For those in recovery, they continue to "work the program," but it is an intellectual and not an emotional exercise. Can people in recovery stay at these identity levels and stay sober? Although we do not want to get into the business of judging the quality of people's recovery, I think the term *dry drunk* appropriately describes many people who do not positively resolve the identity and intimacy stages of development. From my experience, they can continue to live addiction-free but sobriety is much more than not using the substance. Persons who are stuck at these levels are similar to the dry drunk in that they fail to take a good look at themselves and work to give up defenses which keep them from freely accepting and loving themselves and others. I think this difference becomes even more apparent as the individual attempts to have intimate (sexual/romantic) relationships.

How can we deal with this failure to move positively on to the next stage? Not very easily because there is nothing very obviously wrong. There is no concrete problem. Look how bad it had to get before our clients did something about a behavior that was killing them! Addicts are used to feeling so bad that feeling relatively good becomes "good enough" or, as we say in the addiction field, they think "better *is* healthy." If people return to a compulsive behavior, you can work on that because it is tangible. But if people simply do not want to work on moving forward to gain greater feelings of self-acceptance, there is little more we can do. This is a good time to temporarily suspend treatment so that the client can test out his new behaviors and see what he feels is missing.

People find it very difficult to imagine a developmental stage beyond the one they are in. Sometimes we can involve clients in change if their spouse or lover is,threatening to leave them, but this too is tricky because they often blame the spouse and deny that they are part of the problem. Moreover, the problem is not yet an issue of couples therapy, it is an issue for individual or group therapy. You wind up with a couples issue because the recovering individual denies it is his problem. Until the client works through this identity stage, he will not achieve self-acceptance nor will he find the "mature love" promised in the next stage. The intimacy stage will find a negative resolution in the form of isolation or co-dependence.

Stage VII: Intimacy in Love Relationships

As with the previous stage, counseling the client in this stage is not very different from counseling a nonrecovering individual with an intimacy problem. The psychosocial crisis of this stage is intimacy versus isolation. The strength to emerge from the positive resolution of this stage is mature love. The resolution of this stage often occurs between year three and year five. A discussion of how to help clients develop intimate relationships is beyond the scope of this book. However, I hope to give the reader an idea of how to assess and talk about the client's level of intimacy within relationships.

Some issues show up more often in recovering clients. Often childhood sexual abuse will show up at this point. The client may have been acting out sexually her whole life as a way of not getting close to another person. When she stops acting out sexually and stops using drugs and alcohol to not feel, she begins to recall the childhood sexual abuse. Once she works through her feelings about this abuse, her capacity for intimacy increases.

Another problem comes up when your client was married to the same person prior to getting sober and now in sobriety. The spouse married a dysfunctional person (your client), which practically guaranteed there would be no intimacy. The spouse, then, has his own issues with intimacy and if he does not work on them along with his wife, then the relationship is not going to be intimate. This is extremely frustrating for the client who is working so hard to have an intimate relationship. She can do one of three things: accept that she is not going to experience intimacy, wait and hope that the spouse will change, or get out of the marriage. Your client can learn to detach from a spouse who causes her pain, through counseling and self-help groups (e.g., Al-Anon), but detachment is not intimacy. She is still left with a nonintimate relationship.

New intimate relationships are somewhat easier to negotiate. Your client has worked on himself and is now ready to find a partner who is as committed to intimacy as he is. Now that the person has a better developed sense of self, she is less likely to be attracted to an unhealthy person. And, because she has become healthier, she is also less likely to attract an unhealthy person.

How can we help our client move on and positively resolve this final stage? Again, it is never easy and it is sometimes not possible. Since intimacy is itself a vague term, we need to begin by concretely defining intimacy and by asking the client about his feelings concerning the quality of his relationships. Most of our clients will say they don't even know what love is, to say nothing of the concept of intimacy. Another common problem is that they have for so long been the caretakers in relationships, they do not even know what to ask for in terms of intimacy. Many are from broken or dysfunctional homes so there was no modeling of intimacy. They do not have a standard against which to measure the intimacy of their relationships. In helping to educate yourself and the client as to intimate versus nonintimate behaviors, one of the most useful concepts and scales of intimacy is that developed by White (1989) and described as follows.

Intimacy Scale

Several components of an intimate relationship from this intimacy measure are: orientation, caring/concern, sexuality (relevant only for sexually intimate relationships), commitment, and communication/openness. These components are assessed through an open-ended interview (Appendix D) and the responses are then categorized according to level. Using this interview can help you identify the level of functioning of a long-term relationship and can also help identify an addictive versus healthy new relationship. Evaluating the intimacy in a relationship is also helpful for partners who are considering getting married or for married partners who are considering having children.

Each component is scored individually on developmental scales ranging from a low stage 1 to a high stage 6. The six stages can be grouped into three developmental levels: low, medium, and high and these levels are labeled self-focused, role-focused, and individuated-connected. One important assumption within this concept is that one's level of maturity may differ across relationships. For instance, a client may have a more mature relationship with one intimate other (e.g., a spouse) than with another (e.g., a same-sex friend).

Level 1: Self-focused.   The individual at this level sees the partner as a means to selfish end or as an obstacle to those ends. Descriptions of the other are as a source of supply or as a hostile rival for supplies. At this level there is no acknowledgment of the other's equality or separateness, little or no concept of the other's views or feelings. Descriptions of the relationship focus on the subject's own needs (which may be described in glowing detail), and on the partner's success or failure in meeting those needs, but not on the processes internal to the relationship. For some clients at this level, the quality of description may indicate a paucity of inner experience and a feeling of interior emptiness. Extreme dependency on the other, which may take a hostile form, is one possible manifestation of a Level 1 relationship.

Level 2: Role-focused.   At this intermediate level individuals have a basic understanding that the other has needs and feelings too, but their descriptions of relationships lack complexity and depth. Responses rated at the conventional level tend to focus on concrete, external things as the source of problems or as the way to express support. For example: "The only thing I'd like to change in the relationship is to have a better work schedule and be making more money," or "I hug him and kiss him and make sure his dinner is cooked and he has clean clothes to wear to work." "He pays the bills and makes sure the car is running."

Descriptions of the relationship take on the form of stereotyped images of a happy marriage. They are socially acceptable responses, lacking in specific examples that demonstrate an appreciation of the partner's individuality. Role-focused responses lack introspection, and there is a tendency to generalize. The role-focused individual lacks an imaginative, intuitive sense of what it is like to be inside the other's skin. He or she needs to have the partner's needs or feelings spelled out. For example: "I used to get upset about how bitchy she was when I came home from work, but she explained to me how ragged she gets after being with the kids all day, and now I try to take that into account." Many relationships at this level are comfortable and happy, with both partners carrying out roles that society expects from good citizens.

Level 3: Individuated-Connected. The rating denotes that intimate behavior goes beyond a stereotyped, socially acceptable format, with a resulting depth of connection. A mature ability to cope with disappointment, tolerate struggles, and make compromises must be evident. An answer that convincingly demonstrates that conflicts in the relationship are faced and dealt with, and which goes on to express satisfaction and even joy in the partnership, would qualify as highly intimate. There must be evidence that a free choice is made to be close with the specific partner, a choice made from a position of autonomy, rather than out of need or convenience. The client should demonstrate the ability to recognize the partner's individuality, to appreciate the other's unique qualities, and to take pleasure in enhancing the development of the other's talents and powers.

At this level, clients refer to more than the concrete, visible signs of the relationship's quality. They have a concern with the emotional and even spiritual satisfactions to be gained from intimacy with this particular partner. They demonstrate a willingness to pay a lot of attention to "our relationship" and how it is going.

The role-focused level of intimacy describes the type discussed in Stage V, intimacy specific to sobriety. Most of your client's relationships with other A.A. members are role-focused in that they are limited to, or defined by, the A.A. setting and program and do not extend beyond that role. As with marital relationships, these may be happy and comfortable but they are limited because they are role-defined, e.g., the only bond in the relationship may be sobriety. Intimate relationships with the opposite sex (spouse, lover) may also role-defined and this gets in the way of appreciating and facilitating each other's development. The spouse may not complain about, and may even encourage, her recovering spouse to attend more meetings, but she is threatened by those behaviors that do not conform to her concept of recovery. For example, she may get angry at her spouse for his meditation routine because it excludes her and because she does not value that element of recovery.

Stage VII Tasks

This stage of intimacy is more about relationship process than about recovery tasks. The client is maintaining her recovery program and she is vigilant to the possibility of developing substitute addictions. She is learning what her needs are and how to get those needs met in intimate relationships. She is learning how to give up old unhealthy relationships and how to choose new healthy partners. She is working on accepting nonperfection in others (and in herself in relation to others). She is working on being less self-focused and she is learning how to take the perspective of another (put herself in the other's shoes) in order that she develop a *mutual* relationship where both partners can get their needs met.

Resistance and Solutions

As with the prior stage of identity development, there is little you can do to facilitate a person's development of intimacy if he does not identify it as a problem. If your client identifies it as a problem but his spouse does not and the spouse is not willing to work on the relationship, then there is little your client can do other than accept the relationship, hope for a change in the future, or give up the relationship in hopes of finding a more intimate partner. If it is your client who does not want to work on intimacy (but her partner does) then there is little more you can do other than help her get in touch with her feelings about their relationship, such as her feelings about her partner's dissatisfaction with the relationship. Couples counseling or therapy would be a good referral for a client and spouse who are willing to work on achieving intimacy in their relationship.

From my experience, I do not find that a lack of mature love necessarily leads the client back to the use of a chemical, although the client does tend to go through phases of addictive behaviors: food, nicotine, sex. Her ability to "settle" for "less" in a relationship is no different than the nonrecovering person's tendency to do so. This level is called role-focused or conventional because it is just that: the norm that most people in our society develop to, but not beyond.

What I see is happening typically, is the recovering person attempts to positively resolve this stage. She then finds it either too threatening to give up the necessary amount of control or finds a partner unwilling or unavailable. She then re-focuses to self and identity development in the form of furthering her education and career (or that of her children).This development is less threatening because it is something she can do on her own and she does not need to put her feelings on the line in order to achieve success. In terms of relationships, the person continues to be self-focused, co-dependent, and emotionally isolated. On the positive side, there is always the possibility that, in time, the client will feel safe enough to take the risks needed to move on to a positive resolution of the intimacy stage.

13

Conclusion: What Is Recovery?

I n discussing this question with my colleagues, we were pretty clear about what recovery was not. We agreed that clearly recovery is a lot more than not abusing a substance. It is more than identifying oneself as recovering. It is more than attending a Twelve Step program and "working the program." But that is what it is not. We still hadn't come up with what it is? Well, we asked, "What is health?" Being healthy means more than not being sick. Being healthy means taking responsibility for your life, being curious and creative, moving forward positively to discover new things, enjoying yourself in the moment, loving and being loved, and experiencing acceptance of self and others. Recovery is health.

We decided that, as a society, we are addicted to being sick. Most of the clients we see perceive themselves as being sick and professionals too often reinforce this belief. Much of moving on with recovery has to do with giving up the sick, dependent role. This is not just a problem of the addictions field but a problem of the mental health and medical fields. More and more people are being labeled as mentally ill and more and more people are being given "drug therapy" as a cure. Decades ago, Freud prescribed the use of cocaine for his patients, ten years or so ago the "miracle nonaddictive" drug Xanax was in vogue, and today it is the "wonder" drug Prozac. We discover too late that a psychological dependence is as difficult to shake as a physical dependence. Some continue to believe that there is a quick fix for years of abuse on the person.

This is not to say that some people are not mentally ill, and this is not to say that some people do not need medication. Some are and some do. In fact, it is just as harmful to go to the other extreme and damn people for taking a medication they need. Most often, however, clients have simply responded normally to an abusive situation. For instance, being beaten up by a spouse for fifteen years would cause one to feel sad and depressed. Using pills and heroin to deal with life since the age of seventeen would cause one to have difficulty with feelings and boundaries. A recent study reported that the cause of depression in women in our society had more to do with the social conditions (stress of being a female in our society) than conditions inherent in the person. This does not surprise me. We cannot cure a sick society by blaming and medicating its individual members.

Our society continues to be unhealthy and we better teach people that it is unhealthy and that they need to learn how to deal with the craziness of our society lest they become crazy themselves or become society's next scapegoats. The philosophy of teaching clients to live "rationally in an irrational world" was first introduced by Albert Ellis; it is a philosophy I teach my clients and students. Ellis's books and rational humor are wonderful antidotes against a "sick" frame of mind.

Clients are afraid to say "I am healthy" for then they would need to give up their dependency on others and take responsibility for their lives. Taking responsibility means, for them, doing everything perfectly. Clients have said: "I am not as healthy as you think!" What they mean is: "I am not perfect and, therefore, I am too sick to deal with life."

I discover that we, as parents and a society, teach children "It's my way or the highway!" This message encourages their helplessness and dependency as the child is forced to choose either mindless obedience or abandonment by the parent. Those who "choose" the "highway," i.e., leave home, are no less dependent than those who stay, they are simply angrier. The "highway" quickly becomes the "high way" as their dependency needs catch up with them and they pick up their first drug or drink. We teach our children that the only way to connect with people, and be cared for, is by being mindless, sick, dependent. "I am too sick" is their excuse for not dealing with a society that overwhelms them. And "not dealing" with society means not getting anything out of life, for if you shrink from life, you do nothing more than occupy less and less space. We need to teach our clients (and children) that what is important is that you try, not that you succeed. We need to teach that individualism is more important than perfectionism and making mistakes only makes you human.

If anything, the treatment field has become more focused on sickness than ever before. My colleagues and I decided that recovery is a journey from sickness to health. Recovering people need to do more than identify themselves as recovering; they need to integrate that identity into one that defines them as unique and creative individuals. I hope that as professional helpers and parents, we begin to take the focus off sickness and begin to encourage and celebrate individuality and wellness.

Appendix A

THE TWELVE STEPS OF ALCOHOLICS ANONYMOUS

1. We admitted we were powerless over alcohol—that our lives had become unmanageable.
2. Came to believe that a Power greater than ourselves could restore us to sanity.
3. Made a decision to turn our will and our lives over to the care of God *as we understood Him.*
4. Made a searching and fearless moral inventory of ourselves.
5. Admitted to God, to ourselves, and to another human being the exact nature of our wrongs.
6. Were entirely ready to have God remove all these defects of character.
7. Humbly asked Him to remove our shortcomings.
8. Made a list of all persons we had harmed, and became willing to make amends to them all.
9. Made direct amends to such people wherever possible, except when to do so would injure them or others.
10. Continued to take personal inventory and when we were wrong promptly admitted it.
11. Sought through prayer and meditation to improve our conscious contact with God, *as we understood Him,* praying only for knowledge of His will for us and the power to carry that out.
12. Having had a spiritual awakening as the result of these steps, we tried to carry this message to alcoholics, and to practice these principles in all our affairs.

Introduction to
Appendices B, C, and D

The Appendices are included to further the reader's application of the information provided. Appendix B includes sample treatment plans for both inpatient and outpatient setting—with the outpatient treatment plan covering a period of two years of sobriety. From day one we need to know where we want the person to be at year two of recovery in order to provide a meaningful map to reaching that goal. Appendix C provides a sample Return-to-Work agreement so that the reader may see what components need to be included in such an agreement if it is to be successful.

Appendix D is an Intimacy Maturity Interview. I have included this form because I find that many people, including professional helpers, do not know how to talk with clients about intimacy. They do not possess a language of intimacy and, therefore, do not know what to look for in helping clients assess intimacy in their relationships. Developing the capacity for intimacy within a person and within a relationship appears to be the most difficult challenge of later recovery. Having a means of communicating with the client about intimacy is a beginning to facilitating its development.

Appendix B

SAMPLE TREATMENT PLANS

Inpatient

Problem 1:   Chemical dependency

Objective (goal): Sobriety maintenance

Method: 1. No use of alcohol/drugs
2. Attend A.A./N.A.

Objective (goal): Understand disease of addiction

Method: 1. Psychoeducation: read Steps 1, 2, 3 and "Merry-go-Round"
2. Assess knowledge of biological/psychological components of alcohol
3. Learn to access A.A. and understand program:
   a) Obtain telephone numbers
   b) Obtain temporary sponsor

Objective (goal): Understand addiction as pertains to self

Method: 1. Written assignments
   a) Good-bye letter to drug/alcohol
   b) Life-o-gram
   c) Collage
   d) Daily structure log
2. Increase verbalization/participation in peer group, recovery plan developed
3. Identify high risk situations, craving triggers
4. Identify path of progression leading to present admission

Objective (goal): Decrease denial

Method: Increase participation in peer group
       Elicit feedback from group members
       Meet 1:1 with each of other residents

Problem 2:   Decreased capacity to cope with stress

Objective (goal): Learn tolerance of uncomfortable feelings

Method:
1. Develop relaxation skills/ relaxation excercises
2. Use guided imagery
3. Write in a journal
4. Seek out others to talk through uncomfortable feelings
5. Identify sources of stress and coping capacity

Outpatient

Individual Treatment Plan (First Three Months in Treatment)

Problem 1: Chemical dependency

Date identified _____ Date resolved _____
Expected achievement date _____ Date achieved _____

Objective 1: Sobriety maintenance

Method(s): Attend A.A./N.A. 3X/week (ongoing)
     Join a group (target time: 1 month)
     Get and utilize a sponsor (target time: 1 month)
     Individual and group Therapy (ongoing)

Objective 2: Sober environment at home

Method(s): Either have husband move out or have client find
     a sober house or apartment with sober roommate
     (target time: prearranged for discharge date)

Objective 3: Develop return-to-work agreement

Method(s):   Return-to-work agreement (with restrictions)
                   to be signed by client, employer and counselor
              Follow-through with contract conditions
                   (target time: 1 to 3 months)

Was the client involved in the incorporation of this problem
in the treatment plan? _____ Yes _____ No   Explain: _____

_____

Staff member: _____ Client: _____

* * *

Individual Treatment Plan (Three to Six Months)

Problem 1:   Chemical dependency

Date identified _____ Date resolved _____
Expected achievement date _____ Date achieved _____

Objective 1: Sobriety maintenance

Method(s):   No change, continue with plan:
              A.A./N.A., individual, group

Objective 2: Increase socialization/leisure-time activity

Method(s):   Introduce self to two new members at each
                   meeting and get phone numbers
              Ask someone out for coffee (same-sex)
              Go to a movie with a friend

Objective 3: Building trustworthy relationships

Method(s):   Take a risk in group counseling by sharing
                   something you find difficult to accept
                   about yourself
              Give someone in the group feedback about
                   your feelings toward them

Was the client involved in the incorporation of this problem
in the treatment plan? _____ Yes _____ No   Explain: _____

_____

Staff member: _____ Client: _____

* * *

Individual Treatment Plan (Six to Twelve Months)

Problem 1: Chemical dependency

Date identified _____ Date resolved _____
Expected achievement date _____ Date achieved _____

Objective 1: Sobriety maintenance

Method(s): Utilize sponsor more often
Express anger toward sponsor
If conflict not resolvable, find new sponsor
and discuss issues with old sponsor

Objective 2: Resolve marital problems

Method(s): If husband does not have a plan for getting
sober, discuss separation (emotional) from
husband

Objective 3: Identifying and expressing feelings

Method(s): Discuss in individual and then in group,
situations where you felt shame (versus guilt)
Let someone close to you know when he hurt you

Objective 4: Discuss client's level of comfort at work and
consider reducing restrictions or taking a
leave of absence.

Was the client involved in the incorporation of this problem
in the treatment plan? _____ Yes _____ No   Explain: _____

_____

Staff member: _____ Client: _____

* * *

Individual Treatment Plan (Year Two)

Problem 1: Chemical dependency

Date identified ———————————— Date resolved ——————

Expected achievement date ————————— Date achieved ——————

Objective 1: Continue with sobriety maintenance plan

Objective 2: Continue to work on marital issues

Method(s): Discuss effects of emotional and physical abuse
by husband on self-esteem
Discuss feelings of helplessness and hopelessness
Possible grieving of lost relationship with
husband (if husband sober, discuss couples
counseling)

Objective 3: Continue to work on self-esteem

Method(s): Further development of relationships
Possible return for further education, getting
self in shape physically, pursuing a hobby,
taking art classes, etc.
Identifying and speaking up for her rights, e.g.,
assertiveness with boss

Objective 4: Begin to discuss adult child and sexual abuse
issues

Method(s): Discuss in individual and then group counseling
Go to ACOA meeting
Learn to identify co-dependent behavior

Objective 5: Begin to discuss relapse plan and termination issues

Was client involved in the incorporation of this problem
in the treatment plan? ————— Yes ————— No Explain: ———

_____

Staff member: ————————————— Client: —————————————

Appendix C

RETURN-TO-WORK AGREEMENT
BETWEEN
_____ AND _____

The following is a review of the conditions for my return
to work as discussed in our meeting of _____.

1. I will remain drug and alcohol free.
2. I will continue active treatment at Lexington Recovery
   Associates (LRA).
3. LRA will do an ongoing assessment of my progress in
   rehabilitation, as well as urine screens.
4. If it has been determined that I am in relapse, LRA will
   inform _____.
5. I give general permission for _____ to
   contact LRA if s(he) suspects any abuse. LRA staff
   will do an assessment of my status and notify _____
   _____ of any findings.
6. I will maintain contact with _____ for the
   purpose of support and assessment. I give permission for
   random urine screens to be called for by _____.
7. A copy of this agreement will be held by _____.

The date of _____ is established as my reentry date at
_____ on a full time/part time (day/week)
schedule. On _____ it will be determined by LRA and
_____ as to an increase in hours worked per week.

No access to or administration of addictive drugs is permitted
at this time. Reinstatement of medication passing privileges
will be determined by LRA and _____.

It is also understood that I will be working eight-hour shifts and
I will not be working alone.

If I do not follow the above expectations or have any serious job performance difficulties, disciplinary action may occur.

Comments: _____

_____

I have read and understand this agreement and freely give my consent to its implementation.

This agreement will automatically expire: _____.

_____   _____   _____

LRA representative   Employer   Client

Appendix D

The following intimacy maturity interview is the male form, for those married or living with someone. The form for females and forms for males and females not involved with a member of the opposite sex, as well as the scoring manual for the Intimacy Scale, can be obtained by writing to: Kathleen M. White, Ed.D. Boston University, Department of Psychology, 64 Cummington Street, Boston, MA 02215.

Intimacy Maturity Interview
(Male, married or living with someone)

Basically we're interested in learning about people's closest relationships with members of the same and opposite sex. Let's start with the relationship you consider to be your closest.

Who would this be? How long have you been close?

Would you briefly describe this person? What is she like?

What is her view of you?

What kinds of activities do the two of you do separately? (yourself) (her)

> How do you feel when your wife (girlfriend) gets involved in outside or separate activities? Why?

> How does your wife (girlfriend) feel when you get involved in outside or separate activities? Why?

> Do you mind it when your wife (girlfriend) takes on new activities or interests? Why?

> Does your wife (girlfriend) mind it when you take on new activities or interests? Why?

What kinds of things do the two of you usually talk about together? (Do you share worries and problems?)

Do you talk about your relationship with one another? What things concerning your relationship do you talk about?

Do you share problems or differences within the relationship?

(If interviewee says we don't have problems, use optional probes)

How are these dealt with? Why this way?

Who usually initiates efforts to deal with such problems? If unequal, why?

How do you react when she brings up problems or concerns to you about your relationship? Why?

How does she react when you bring up problems or concerns to her about your relationship? Why?

Are there any ways in which you could be more open with her?

Are there any ways in which she could be more open with you?

Optional Probes for the above section on disclosure and communication.

People sometimes get on each other's nerves in some way or another. Is there anything about your wife (girlfriend) that you dislike? Have you discussed this with him/her?

Is there anything about yourself that gets on your wife's (girlfriend's) nerves? Has she expressed this to you?

Do you ever have any fights? How do they usually get started? How do the two of you deal with such differences?

What ways do you show your wife (girlfriend) you care about her?

Would she like you to express you caring differently?

What ways does your wife (girlfriend) show she cares about you?

Would you like her to express her caring differently?

(Do you do things for each other without being asked or go out of your way to help?)

Would your wife (girlfriend) say you are as concerned about her needs as your own? If no, why?

In regards to the sexual side of the relationship, are you satisfied with the way things are?

Is your wife (girlfriend) satisfied with the sexual side of your relationship?

As a couple, have you discussed the sexual aspect of your relationship with each other? Explain.

How frequently do you have such discussions?

Would you like to see anything change? Explain.

How do you think she would view these changes?

Would your wife (girlfriend) like to see any changes? Explain.

What do you think of these changes?

Overall, have there been any important changes in your sexual relations?

How have you reacted to these changes?

How has she?

In reference to your relationship overall, does one of you show more involvement than the other? If yes, why so and is this a source of difficulties?

How committed to this relation are you? Your wife (girlfriend)?

Do you ever feel in conflict about this relationship?

Do you ever think about alternatives to your present relation?

Given that every relation has room to grow, how could you contribute to improving the general quality of your relationship as it currently exists?

References

Alcoholics Anonymous. 1985. *Alcoholics Anonymous* (3rd ed.). New York: Alcoholics Anonymous World Services.

American Psychiatric Association. 1987. *Diagnostic and Statistical Manual of Mental Disorders. Third Edition. Revised.* Washington, DC: American Psychiatric Association.

Beattie, M. 1987. *Co-Dependent No More.* Center City, MN: Hazelden Foundation.

Benjamin, A. 1974. *The Helping Interview* (2nd Ed.). Boston; Houghton, Mifflin Co.

Bissell, L., and Royce, J. E. 1987. *Ethics for Addiction Professionals.* Center City, MN: Hazelden Foundation.

Black, C. 1981. *It Will Never Happen to Me.* Denver: M.A.C. Printing and Publications Division.

Bohman, M. 1978. Some genetic aspects of alcoholism and criminality. *Archives of General Psychiatry*, 35, 269–276.

Bradshaw, J. 1988. *Healing the Shame That Binds You.* Deerfield Beach, FL: Health Communications.

Carey, K. B., and Maisto, S. A. 1985. A review of the use of self-control techniques in the treatment of alcohol abuse. *Cognitive Therapy and Research*, 9, 235–251.

Carkhuff, R. R. 1987. *The Art of Helping VI.* Amherst, MA: Human Resource Development Press.

Cermak, T. L. 1986. *Diagnosing and Treating Co-Dependence.* Minneapolis, MN: Johnson Institute Books.

Daley, D. C., Moss, H., and Campbell, F. 1987. *Dual Disorders.* Center City, MN: Hazelden Foundation.

Ellis, A. 1962. *Reason and Emotion in Psychotherapy.* Secaucus, NJ: Citadel Press.

Ellis, A. 1972. *Psychotherapy and the value of a human being.* New York: Institute for Rational-Emotive Therapy.

Ellis, A. 1975. *How to Live with a Neurotic: At home and at work.* New York: Crown (rev. ed., Hollywood, CA: Wilshire, 1975).

Ellis, A. 1977a. Fun as psychotherapy. *Rational Living*, 12(1), 2–6.

Ellis, A. 1977b. (Speaker). *A Garland of Rational Humorous Songs*. (Cassette recording). New York: Institute for Rational Living.

Ellis, A., McInerney, J., DiGiuseppe, R., and Yeager, R. 1988. *Rational-Emotive Therapy with Alcoholics and Substance Abusers*. New York: Pergamon Press.

Erikson, E. H. 1968. *Childhood and Society*. New York: W. W. Norton & Co.

Erikson, E. H. 1982. *The Life Cycle Completed*. New York: W. W. Norton & Co.

Freud, S. 1943. *A General Introduction to Psychoanalysis*. New York: Doubleday.

Glasser, W. 1965. *Reality Therapy: A New Approach to Psychiatry*, New York: Harper & Row.

Glasser, W. 1976. *Positive Addiction*. New York: Harper & Row.

Gonsiorek, J. 1987. Treatment of the therapist, In G. Schoener, J. Milgrom, J. Gonsiorek, E. Luepker, and R. Conroe (eds.), *Psychotherapists' Sexual Involvement with Clients: Intervention and prevention*. Minneapolis, MN: Walk-in Counseling Center.

Goodwin, D. W. 1976. *Is Alcoholism Hereditary?* New York: Oxford University Press.

Gorski, T., and Miller, M. 1982. *Learning to Live Again: Guidelines for Recovery*. Independence, MO: Herald House.

Hansen, J. C., Stevic, R. R., and Warner, R. W. 1977. *Counseling*. Boston, MA: Allyn and Bacon.

Hester, R. K., and Miller, W. R. (eds.). 1989. *Handbook of Alcoholism Treatment Approaches*. New York: Pergamon Press.

Jellinek, E. M. 1960. *The Disease Concept of Alcoholism*. New Haven, CT: Hill House Press.

Jellinek, E. M. 1962. Phases of alcohol addiction. In D. J. Pittman and S. R. Snyder (eds.), *Society, Culture, and Drinking Patterns*. New York: John Wiley & Sons.

Kinney, J., and Leaton, G. 1983. *Loosening the Grip*. St. Louis, MO: The C. V. Mosby Company.

Kübler-Ross, E. 1969. *On Death and Dying*. New York: Macmillan Publishing Co.

Marlatt, G. A. 1983. The controlled drinking controversy: A commentary. *American Psychologist*, (10), 1097–1110.

Maslow, A. 1970. *Motivation and Personality*, (2nd ed.). New York: Harper & Row.

Maultsby, M. C. 1978. *The Rational Behavioral Alcoholic-Relapse Prevention Treatment Method*. Lexington, KY: Rational Self-Help Aids.

Miller, P. M. 1976. A comprehensive behavioral approach to the treatment of alcoholism. In Ralph Tarter and A. Arthur Sugerman (eds.), *Alcoholism: Interdisciplinary Approaches to an Enduring Problem.* Reading, MA: Addison-Wesley Publishing Co.

Pope, K. S., and Bouhoutsos, J. 1986. *Sexual Intimacy Between Therapists and Patients.* New York: Praeger.

Rippere, V., and Williams, R. (eds.). 1985. *Wounded Healers: Mental Health Workers' Experiences of Depression.* New York: John Wiley & Sons.

Rogers, C. R. 1951. *Client-Centered Therapy.* Boston: Houghton-Mifflin.

Rogers, C. R. 1961. *On Becoming a Person.* Boston: Houghton-Mifflin.

Schoener, G. 1987. Assessment and development of rehabilitation plans for the therapist. In G. Schoener, J. Milgrom, G. Gonsiorek, E. Luepker, and R. Conroe (eds.), *Psychotherapists' Sexual Involvement with Clients: Intervention and Prevention.* Minneapolis, MN: Walk-in Counseling Center.

Trimpey, Jack. 1990. Rational Recovery: a bold new approach to addiction care. *The Humanist,* January/February. Amherst, NY: American Humanism Association.

Truax, C., and Carkhuff, R. 1967. *Toward Effective Counseling and Psychotherapy.* Chicago: Aldine Publishing Co.

White, K. 1989. *Intimacy Scoring Manual.* In press, Social Science Document Service.

Yalom, I. D. 1985. *The Theory and Practice of Group Psychotherapy.* (3rd ed.). New York: Basic Books.